HERBS, GREENS, FRUIT

The key to the Mediterranean diet

10657554

TITLE

HERBS, GREENS, FRUIT
The key to the Mediterranean diet

AUTHOR

Myrsini Lambraki

COPYRIGHT

Myrsini Lambraki

Raftopoulou Sr. 31,

71305 Heraklion, Crete

TEL.& FAX: +30-81-210.052 & 346.554

MOBILE PHONE: 0945. 468190

E-MAIL: mirsini@her.forthnet.gr

web site://users.forthnet.gr/her/mi

FIRST EDITION
May 2001

ISBN: 960-91513-4-5

TRANSLATION

George Trialonis, Tel:+30-81-341832

PHOTOGRAPHS

Douwe Hoogstins

Panagiotis Beltzinitis, Myrsini Lambraki

LAYOUT

MKS Metaxaraki Advertising

❧ ❧ ❧

All rights reserved.
No part of this publication may be reproduced,
stored in a retrieval system or transmitted in any form
or by any means, electronic, mechanical, photocopying,
recording or otherwise, without prior permission
of the editor. Law 2121/1993 and regulations of
International Law that apply in Greece

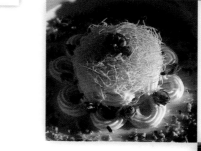

MYRSINI LAMBRAKI

HERBS, GREENS, FRUIT

The key to the Mediterranean diet

100 Recipes
& *30* Beverages

Table of Contents

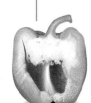

Damaskus-Rose

WHAT ARE HERBS?

According to the Oxford dictionary herbs are all the useful plants whose leaves, roots, stems and flowers are valued as food or medicines by dint of their aroma or other characteristic. This definition applies to a wide variety of plants that are used in food, drinks, medicines, cosmetics, etc. However, in the last few centuries the term "herb" has been reserved strictly for a limited range of plants attributed with medicinal qualities and used for infusions, popular treatments, or as raw material in modern pharmacology.

HERBS AND THEIR MEDICINAL VALUE

The distinction of plants into herbs, vegetables, greens, and fruits is only a few centuries old. In antiquity, even up to the Middle Ages, the Greeks, Romans, Arabs, Chinese and the Hindus, attributed to plants therapeutic qualities and included them in their daily diet. Plants were consumed raw or cooked and combined with fish and meat dishes. In any case, it has been proved that the above plant categories maintain their active ingredients and therapeutic qualities even when cooked.

The Cretan nutritional model includes a wide range of plants (wild greens, vegetables, fruit and seeds) known as "herbs of the kitchen". This qualification is used with the implication that these herbs, if consumed daily, promote health and long life. For a cook in ancient Greece or in the Middle Ages, the lettuce, saffron, bulbs, asparagus, radishes, even pomegranates and berries were in the same plant category as sage, marjoram, and dittany, although the former were not used for infusions. Extracts from ancient Greek texts prove that most greens, vegetables, fruit and herbs were attributed effective therapeutic qualities. Hesiod, for example, was urging the Athenians to consume nettles to shield themselves from common ailments for an entire year.

Centuries later, John Evelyn (1699) wrote, "It [the borage] is known to enliven the spirit of hypochondriacs and relieve the mind of people steeped in study …". Borage was used in salads, as is the case today. Charlemagne, king of the Franks (742-814 AD) commissioned the compilation of a list of the most valued aromatic herbs and named the list "friend of the physician and the pride of the cook". He then ordered that the herbs on that list be grown in his lush gardens.

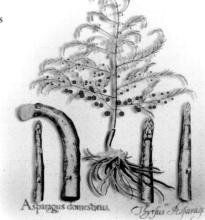
Asparagus domesticus. Byrsus Asparag.

THE MYTH OF GODDESS FLORA

The bonds between our ancestors and nature (mainly plants) is not only testified by volumes of specialist works and literary extracts but also by myths, as is the case with the myth of the goddess of vegetation, Flora. In his book "The Flora of Greece", chapter "Myth and Cult", E. Bauman provides a wonderful description of the connection between nature, gods and people: "Goddess Flora was assisted in her tasks by the Horae (or Hours) the daughters of goddess Themis and Zeus and attendants to the Sun. The Horae were the three goddesses of seasons and of orderliness. Zephyr, representing the west wind, brought the Spring rains that were so valuable for the awakening of nature. The Oceanids, nymphs and daughters of Oceanus and Tethys, were protectors of their father's marine kingdom and cared for all sea and river plant life. Where the nymphs were unable to attend, there Zeus rolled his thunders and lightning from the heights of Olympus, thus wetting fields and meadows with rain. Artemis (Diana), the goddess of the hunt and the moon, would cover plants with evening frost, while her brother Apollo showered plants with the invigorating rays of the sun…"

Modern epidemiologists, physicians, and nutrition experts believe that herbs, wild greens and fresh fruits native to the Mediterranean are "loaded" with solar energy. The sun over the Mediterranean seems to exert a most beneficial influence on all edible plants with subsequent effects on human health.

A statue of an idol from the end of the Minoan period. This goddess is wearing a wreath of poppy heads which symbolize health and fertility.

A lady picking the sprouting ends of the plant before the bud flowers. This part of the plant has taken in plenty of Mediterranean sunshine and therefore is rich in vitality.

Aristotle wrote that when the wild goat was wounded it would eat the Cretan dittany in order to heal itself.

HERBS IN MEDICINE HIPPOCRATES – THEOPHRASTUS – DIOSCURIDES, GALINUS (GALEN)

Through centuries of trial and error activities primitive man became aware of the medicinal qualities of plants and herbs. He identified herbs that could sooth a range of pains and cure diseases or prevent others. A lot of herbs/plants used for their medicinal qualities today, for example the sage, cedar tree, and the leaves of the olive tree, were known to the Egyptians and found inscribed in papyrus scrolls.

For centuries the medicinal applications of herbs/plants were mainly confined to the treatment of wounds, since anything pathological was attributed to acts of gods. This attitude and practice changed with Hippocrates (460-370 BC), the famous Greek physician and father of medicine from the isle of Kos. His works that survived through the centuries include references to 237 plant species classified on the basis of their medicinal qualities. According to Hippocrates, saffron is used for wound cleansing, mallow for cataplasms, oregano to aid menstruation, pomegranate for ailments of the liver, sage for uterus infections and gastrointestinal diseases, Cretan dittany to aid labouring women and on wounds, quince to alleviate pains of the uterus, purslane as a axative, and basil as an antiemetic.

In his work, "On the History of Plants", Theophrastus, the Greek philosopher and scientist (372-287 BC), set the foundations for modern botany. He provides invaluable information concerning the pharmaceutical and aromatic qualities of a wide range of plants. Centuries later botany found its main exponent in the person of Dioscurides (c.512 AD). His knowledge of plants/herbs are astonishing, even to modern standards. In his book "De materia medica", Dioscurides identified more than 500 plant species. Of note is the fact that 40 of these are currently used in pharmacology. The bulk of our knowledge of plants and herbs in ancient Greece comes from the works of Theophrastus and Dioscurides.

At a later time Greek compilations of herbs and plants were systematized by Claudius Galinus (Galen, 131-109 AD), Greek physician and medical writer from Pergamum, Asia Minor. He recorded 304 medicines that were produced from herbs, wild greens, trees and fruits.

With the fall of Rome, all knowledge about herbs/plants that had been accumulated through the previous centuries was disseminated to Byzantium (Constantinople) and the Arab world, particularly to Persia. This knowledge was enriched and supplemented with native knowledge about spices and infusions to be epitomized in the book of Avisenna "Canon of Medicine" which was based on the principles of Galinus. Avisenna was an Iranic Islamic philosopher and physician of the early 11th century AD.

BYZANTIUM – MIDDLE AGES – MODERN TIMES

During the Byzantine period herbs and vegetables were associated with lower the classes social, hence they were rarely served at the dinner tables of the upper class, kings and gourmets. On the other hand, this lowly and inexpensive diet was much appreciated by the common folk, poor and clergy. Harvesting/collection and supplying of herbs and vegetables were highly systematised by the clergy who observed strict fasting rules for almost 180 days during a year.

References to chicory varieties, rocket, mallow, cabbage, leek, spinach, carrot, coriander, cress, lettuce and radish are found in the works of Johannes Konder ("The Gardner and Daily Cuisine in Byzantium" and F. Koukoule ("The Life and Culture of the Byzantines"). In the same works, the rosemary, (spear)mint, fennel, oregano, saffron (colouring agent for vinegar), and pomegranate's juice (particularly of the sour fruit variety) are cited as condiments.

Bafilicum Indicum macu, latum.

During the Middle Ages – notwithstanding the negative associations this period brings to mind – herbs and vegetables flourished in monastery gardens and yards. In this sense the Middle Ages are considered the Golden Age of Botany. It is no accident that pioneering scientists – Paracelsus (Swiss physician and alchemist, 1493–1541), Nicholas Culpeper (English physician, 1616-1654), Parkinson (British physician, 1755–1824), William Turner (English anatomist, 1832-1916), Gérard Encausse (Spanish-born French physician occultist, 1865 - 1916), etc., experimented with standard herbs and others imported from India, the Americas and China.

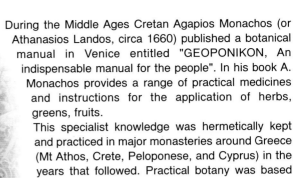

During the Middle Ages Cretan Agapios Monachos (or Athanasios Landos, circa 1660) published a botanical manual in Venice entitled "GEOPONIKON, An indispensable manual for the people". In his book A. Monachos provides a range of practical medicines and instructions for the application of herbs, greens, fruits.

This specialist knowledge was hermetically kept and practiced in major monasteries around Greece (Mt Athos, Crete, Peloponese, and Cyprus) in the years that followed. Practical botany was based on the observation and examination of the lush Greek country side. Approximately 4000 plant species were identified and their medicinal and culinary applications were recorded. Subsequently, this knowledge was disseminated to common folks and practiced widely by housewives in the country-side. Gradually, the term herbs was confined to those plants that, owing to their medicinal qualities, were used only for healing purposes.

WINES WITH HERBS

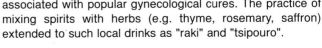

Our ancestors loved to experiment with various tastes and fragrances. They relished fragrant bread, pies stuffed with vege-tables/greens, honey, cheese, wines and herbs.

Residues of wine, raisins, honey and barley were found inside a three-legged urn on Crete dating from 1190-1130 BC. In his manuscript "Singular Tastes of Wine", physician and nutrition expert, Aegimeios (4th c. BC) from Helia provides scores of pie recipes with common wine where the leaves and fruits of sage had been soaked. In addition to the nutritional value of those pies, the ancient expert underlines their curative qualities. Sage infused wine in crocks was exported from the isle of Cyme to Egypt in the beginning of 18th c. BC. This trade yielded significant profits to wine merchants since the wine was heavily priced owing to its therapeutic qualities. In modern Greece wine mixed with sage fruits was associated with popular gynecological cures. The practice of mixing spirits with herbs (e.g. thyme, rosemary, saffron) extended to such local drinks as "raki" and "tsipouro".

FICO comune *(volg.)* Fico albo tondo.

FICUS carica *(Linn.)*

(½ Grand. nat.)

A. Frutto d'autunno. B. Frutto d'estate, o Fico fiore. 1 Taglio verticale di
una placenta turbinata, contenente i fiori maschi e femmine. a. Apertura
con squille. b. Placenta. c. Squamme formanti l'orifizio della placenta. 2.
Fiore maschio. 3. Fiore femmina. 4. Taglio verticale d'una placenta ma-
tura. 5. Frutto. 6. Id. Tagliato per mostrare il seme. 7. Seme. 8. Id. spoglia-
to del tegumento. 9. Id. Tagliato. 10. Embrione.

Herbs – Vegetables – Fruits of Crete

The deceptively barren hills and mountains of Crete, the rocky landscape, thick olive groves, uncultivated plots, even the rugged coastline host a most interesting flora, a unique evolutionary crossbreed of the European, African and Asian flora. Many of the plant species endemic to Crete actually naturalized from other continents centuries ago. In particular, the Cretan flora includes 57 species native of Asia and not found anywhere else in Europe, and 231 species not encountered in mainland Greece.

In 19th century botanist M. Rikli published a list of 28 African plant species endemic to deserts and the steppe, however 8 of those were also recorded on Crete. This explains the enthusiasm of Austrian born physician-botanist F.W. Sieber who visited Crete and later wrote, "…what impressed me most was a leafless and flowerless sprig of the capparis egyptiana. On closer examination of the stem, I concluded that I was looking at a capparis shrub. I identified the Egyptian species of capparis following examination of its golden reflexed spines. This species is not found in Europe."

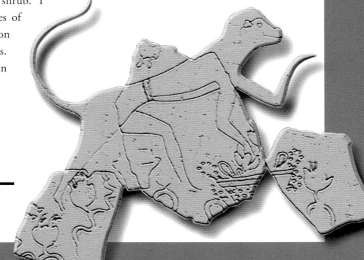

A monkey gathering crocus flowers. From a fresco at the Archaeological Museum in Heraklion.

An elderly Cretan man staring out at the rugged landscape. It is home to a wide variety of herbs and wild greens, like dittany and sage, the key to Cretan longevity.

HERBS – VEGETABLES – FRUITS OF CRETE

In his three volume work "Vegetation of the Mediterranean region", M. Rikli provides a table of plant species encountered in five of the largest islands in the Mediterranean – Sicily, Sardenia, Cyprus, Corsica and Crete. He notes that although Crete is comparatively the smallest of the five, yet it hosts the richest flora of all with more than 2,170 species. The comparison is even more compelling on the basis of the following facts: England, although double in size than Greece, hosts only 2,133 plant species, while prewar Germany and Austria numbered only 3,500 plant species.

Our information about the variety of plant species flourishing during the Minoan period on Crete is very scanty, originating mainly from archaeological excavations which yielded murals and vases with representations of fruit, trees, herbs, etc. Other information comes from paleo-botanist research. However, we should take into account that all living organisms, including plant life, evolve through time. Therefore, known plant species today may be the evolutionary descendants of species that existed in varied forms in the remote past. Identification of past plant species is rather difficult, however, information about their applications can be deduced from their representations on excavated murals and artifacts. A vessel containing vegetable remains was found during excavations at the Minoan palace of Malia. Three kinds of fruits, corresponding to different plant species (cedar tree, coriander, wild fennel) were identified. Even today cedar fruits are consumed by the inhabitants of the isle of Gavdos, south of Crete. Furthermore, the rich aroma of wild fennel is much appreciated by the modern Cretan cuisine.

During the summer of 2000 new excavations at the village of Archanes by Cretan archaeologists Yiannis and Efi Sakelarakis confirmed the belief that aromatic herbs were used and traded by the Minoans. Unearthed vessels of 1 and ½ lt were probably used as containers for the kinds of herbs exported to mainland Greece and Egypt. The Minoans used the saffron crocus in their meals and in rituals. This is testified by mural representations. We now know that

Cingus Geingnsium. Cinara maior Boloni, enfis (inara seu Articbochini jatio.

HERBS – VEGETABLES – FRUITS OF CRETE

the saffron crocus was intensively cultivated and used up to 16th and 17th century. This is supported by the following extract from popular literature, "…Oh! Spaghetti with grated cheese and richly saffroned, …dearest cheese pies …" More information about the plant species of Crete comes from authors, botanists, and physicians of antiquity, e.g. Homer, Theophrastus, Dioscurides, Pliny, Galen, Diodorus and Oreivasius. On the basis of ancient literature and research the following plant species were of outmost importance to the ancients: dittany, the Cretan cypress tree, palm tree, oregano, thyme and the cedar tree.

Claudius Galen, the personal physician of Roman emperor Marcus Aurelius, reports on the unique medicinal qualities of edible Cretan herbs: "Many of the herbs cultivated in the emperor's gardens originate from Crete. Many of the greens, herbs, fruits, and seeds on this island can not be found anywhere in the world…"

However, from 5th to 15th century AD we have very little information about the flora of Crete which comes from Cretan literature, particularly from Cretan theatrical plays. From this information we can deduce that Cretans consumed considerable quantities of wild greens and vegetables: "She either harvested greens from meadows all day, or kneaded, sieved, wove till nightfall." (Chortatsis, "Panoria").

No other flora on earth has been investigated so thoroughly as the flora of the island of Crete. It all started in 15th century when a large number of botanists, pharmacologists, historians and travelers arrived on the island of Crete for a thorough examination of the local flora. French botanist Piere Belon recorded 96 plant species in their original, local names.

By order of the king of France Luis XIV, French traveler-researcher Tournefort traveled east and came to Crete where he recorded 396 plant species. In 1794 one more French traveler, Olivier, arrived on Crete to report, in fascination, that the Cretans used the chickpea's leaves raw in salads and fried the leaves of beans stalks in olive oil.

Dutch physician Dapper, who visited Crete in 17th century, reported a wide range of edible herbs, greens and vegetables, among them the dittany (dictamus) which was also chewed by goats to heal their wounds.

THE NUTRITIONAL VALUE OF WILD GREENS – HERBS AND FRUIT

THE MEDITERRANEAN DIET

In 1999 the National Centre for Nutrition, of the National School for Public Health, headed by Mrs. Antonia Trichopoulou, in collaboration with the Hellenic Chemistry Laboratory and company RTD of of Food Industry (ETAT.S.A.) conducted a large scale research concerning the nutritional value of a group of 17 different wild herbs which were used in cottage pie recipes.

Scientific examination of Cretan pies confirmed the existence of flavonoids, substances of plant origin containing flavone in various combinations (anthoxanthins, apigenins, flavones, quercitins, etc.) and with varying biological activities. These substances are antioxidant and found in fruit and vegetables. Medical research on flavonoids has proven their positive action in preventing cardiovascular diseases and tumor growths. The raw herbs or greens used in Cretan pies are rich in flavonoids while significant amounts are retained even after the pies are cooked. Herbs and greens rich in flavonoids are: the fennel, leek, poppy flower, sorrel and wild carrot.

The green parts of dandelion are rich in vitamin A. The nettle is a significant source of iron and carotene B. The chicory is rich in vitamin B12 which is necessary for cell function. The seeds of the wild rosebush are rich in vitamin C and the carob-beans in proteins. The mint and thyme are characterised by anticeptic and anti-microbial qualities, while sage is used to heal wounds of the oral cavity. The chemical constitution of grapes is similar to mother's milk while the consumption of a glass of red wine protects the arteries of the heart. Fruit provide ample vegetable fibers and minerals which aid the function of the intestines.

EIGHT BASIC POINTS OF THE MEDITERRANEAN DIET

1. High ratio of monounsaturates (olive oil) over saturated lipids (butter, lard).
2. Moderate consumption of alcohol (1-2 glasses of red wine / day)
3. High consumption of greens / vegetables.
4. High consumption of cereals (including whole grain bread)
5. High consumption of fruits.
6. High consumption of herbs
7. Low consumption of meat and related products
8. Low consumption of milk and dairy products.

Individuals who abide by the above eight points are considered to be proportionally closer to the Mediterranean diet and a healthier living.

THE PYRAMID OF THE MEDITERRANEAN DIET

1. Meat
2. Sweets
3. Eggs
4. Potatoes
5. Beans, Legumes and dried fruit
6. Poultry
7. Fish
8. Dairy
9. Olive oil and olives
10. Greens / Vegetables / Herbs / Fruit
11. Pasta, Rice

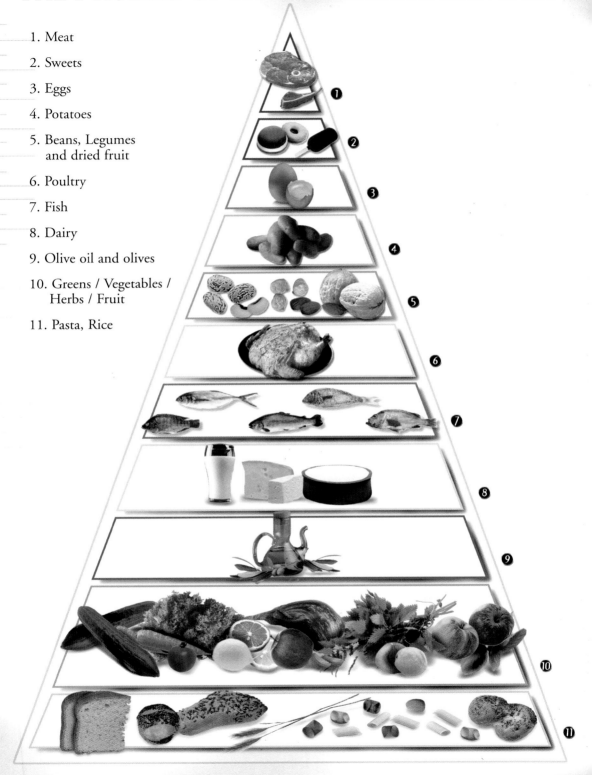

THE ANTIOXIDANT QUALITIES OF HERBS

– OLIVE OIL WITH HERBS –

Vegetable oils scented with herbs and spices were extensively used in antiquity, but we have no knowledge of their application in the kitchen. We do know, however, that owing to their inherent qualities, vegetable oils were used for body care. Selected herbs were added to vegetable oils to lend them valuable curative, styptic and antioxidant qualities.

During the reign of Byzantine emperor Constantine "the purple-born", legist Cassianos Vassos is credited with a number of recipes for scented olive oil. Some of these recipes provide instructions for improving medium and low quality olive oils with the addition of aromatic herbs. For example, rancid olive oil improves with the addition of dill and foul-smelling olive oil with the addition of coriander or raisins. A popular practice in the villages of the province of Pediada, Crete, was to add 2-3 oregano sprigs in large earthenware jars used as olive oil containers.

There has been a lot of research in the plant kingdom for substances with antioxidant qualities, particularly in herbs and aromatic plants, the main sources of antioxidants. Independent investigation results concur on the significant antioxidant qualities of rosemary and oregano.

In 1952 Chipault noted that consumption of salted meat should be combined with infusions of rosemary, sage, and thyme. In addition, he claims that oregano combined with mayonnaise acquires excellent antioxidant properties. Modern research is under way by the Aristotelian University of Athens with regard to the stability of olive oils mixed with rosemary, oregano, garlic and thyme.

TIPS FOR HARVESTING HERBS & WILD PLANTS

The proper harvesting of wild herbs is determined by the particular location of the plants as well as their subsequent culinary application. In particular,

- Leaves, shoots and blossomed tops should be harvested during the afternoon hours when most of the plants' active substances accumulate in those sections. Similarly, roots and bulbs should be collected in autumn or spring, and fruits, flowers early in the morning all year round.
- Never harvest plants/herbs, if you are not sure whether they are edible.
- Herbs and wild greens growing on roadsides or curbs are not suitable for consumption.
- Harvesting during the months of March and April requires caution since during that period most farmers spray their land with hazardous pesticides.
- Harvest only the green and healthier looking herbs/plants.
- Do not uproot herbs/plants, but trim the tender parts to give plants/herbs the opportunity to grow again.
- Harvest only the quantities you consider enough to last you for 5-6 days. Herbs and plants loose their precious qualities after this period.
- Never leave plants/herbs in nylon/plastic bags, closed spaces, under direct sun light or in the trunk of your vehicle.

TIPS FOR PURCHASING HERBS & WILD PLANTS

- If you live in the country, but do not have the knowledge required to identify specific herbs and wild plants, or the time to harvest them yourselves, look for them in your local market or greengrocer.
- It is advisable to find out the origin of the herbs and plants you intend to buy.
- Never purchase herbs/plants with obvious damage on leaves or fruits.

TIPS FOR STORING HERBS & WILD PLANTS

• Wild plants and herbs are best for consumption the same day of purchase. The same is true for all vegetables.

• Never wash or rinse wild plants if you intend to store them in a freezer or refrigerator for a few days. Refrigerated plants turn yellow and give off a foul smell in a week or so. If you must refrigerate wild plants, store them at the lower compartment of the refrigerator.

• Always remove the yellow leaves, soil or any other visible foreign matter before refrigerating herbs and wild plants. Do not wash.

• Wild plants with thick leaves and stems last longer in the freezer/refrigerator. However, chicory and asparagus wither and turn yellow quite easily.

TIPS FOR WASHING HERBS & WILD PLANTS

• Herbs and wild plants should not be soaked or they will loose many of their much desired substances (particularly sugars, vitamins and minerals)

• Always rinse them under running water, particularly the leaves and root section.

• Never dispose of roots since they concentrate valuable substances (water, sugar, etc.) Roots are best cleaned with a brush. Do not scrape them with knives or other sharp instruments.

• Wild plants harvested from areas frequented by sheep and dogs should first be soaked in a vinegar solution for 10 minutes prior to consumption and then rinsed thoroughly.

Salad spinner.

Picking grapes (sultani) in a vineyard.

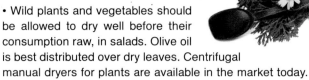

PREPARATION FOR COOKING WILD PLANTS

• Wild plants and vegetables should be allowed to dry well before their consumption raw, in salads. Olive oil is best distributed over dry leaves. Centrifugal manual dryers for plants are available in the market today.

• Wild herbs and vegetables should not be finely chopped when using less than 4 species.

• Do not mash wild plants and vegetables when making wild soups. It is best to chop them finely with a sharp knife.

• To get the most out of wild plants and vegetables, it is best to consume them raw. The more you process foods, the higher the loss of their valuable substances. Boiling wild food for 4 minutes corresponds to 20-45% loss of their minerals and 75% loss of their vitamins.

• Adding an acidic medium, e.g. lemon juice or vinegar, to boiling or raw plants minimizes the loss of vitamins.

• The most popular mode of wild plant preparation is boiling. However, one should take the following tips into consideration:

• allow the water to come to the boil prior to adding the wild plants. This way the plants will not bleach but will retain their beautiful green colour.

• Boil wild plants in as little water as possible: rinse them thoroughly and put them wet in a pot. Mix them well and add a little water.

• Caution: some plants, e.g., chicory, should be boiled in ample water, otherwise they turn yellow. Also, wild and bitter plants should be boiled in ample water to discharge their bitter substances.

• Adding soda to boiling wild plants will help them retain their beautiful colour, however, most of their valuable substances will be lost, particularly vitamin C.

• Add salt to boiling wild plants approximately 8 minutes before you take the pot off the oven ring or before serving.

• Wild plants should be boiled in covered pots at high heat. The longer the cooking time the higher the loss of valuable substances.

• Strain boiled plants the soonest possible, otherwise they will turn yellow.

• You may want to catch the juice from strained boiled wild plants and vegetables to make a healthy drink. Store the juice in glass jars

and refrigerate for 2-3 days. To make a tasty drink, warm the juice and add lemon juice, salt and a little olive oil. The same wild plant juice can be used in soups and sauces.

PRESERVATION / CONSERVATION

• Pickles can also be made from purslane, vineyard offshoots, artichokes, and bulbs. Use extra quality vinegar and olive oil.
• Fruit make nice preserves in alcohol ("raki", vodka, wine) while they provide excellent fragrance to these mediums.
• You can keep wild plants in deep-freezing all year round. Let them soak in water for 10 minutes, then collect them with a perforated spoon and place them into plastic bags. Finally, store them in your freezer.
• The freezer is not the most suitable place to store wild plants and herbs, excepting such aromatic herbs as fennel, leek, poppy, nettle and mallow.
• Frozen wild plants intended for pies should be allowed to thaw at room temperature and then strained.

COLLECTION OF HERBS

This activity requires particular care since it affects the chemical constitution and nutritional value of herbs.

1. Avoid collecting larger quantities than you actually need.
2. Leaves are best before the plant blossoms, while herb fruits and shoots after the plant blossoms.
3. Aromatic herbs should be collected during morning hours (early in the morning, provided there is no frost). Herbs should not be collected when it rains.
4. Use a pair of scissors to cut the tender part of herbs, never uproot them. Uproot only when you require the roots. Roots are best in Autumn, when the plant has stopped the production of leaves and flowers.
Herbs, particularly the marjoram, oregano, sage, (spear)mint, laurel, thyme and rosemary, are usually dried. Leafy herbs, e.g. basil, tend to wither and loose their tasty substances after drying.

DRYING HERBS

The best way to dry herbs is to make little bunches and rig them upside down on a line in a cool, dry and drafty place. Bunches should be thin so that the circulating air can dry the herbs to the core. You may want to cover the bunch with a cloth to prevent accumulation of dust. Make sure that the temperature is steady and the air is dry. Avoid humid areas.

The faster the drying of herbs, the better. Do not dry herbs under direct sun light, or they will wither. The ideal temperature is 20-31oC.
The leaves are dried whole. The drying period depends on the plant itself. Drying delicate leaves requires 3-4 days, while leaves from long-lasting herbs requires 6-8 days. As soon as the herbs are dry, pluck their leaves and place them in airtight jars and store away in a cool, dry place.

Use dried herbs six months later, but not much later since they tend to loose their aroma. The kitchen oven can also be used for drying herbs. It is rather difficult to determine the exact time required for each herb to dry in an oven since herbs vary in constitution and humidity content.
To dry herbs in the kitchen oven you need to place them on a flat baking pan lined with baking sheets or foil and heat them at 50oC. Use your experience and common sense to check if the herbs have reached a satisfactory dry stage before removing them from the oven. Leafy herbs, e.g. the basil, maintain their beautiful green colour when dried in the oven. Should you notice humidity in the glass jars where you have stored herbs, empty the contents of the jars in a baking pan and dry the herbs as above for 8-10 minutes. Store the dried herbs in dry, airtight jars.

An old lady in the Cretan countryside gathering wild oregano which she will then dry and use for traditional dishes and tea. To use fresh oregano, hold the rinsed and dried stems in one hand and strip off the leaves by running your fingers of the other hand down the stems.

PRESERVATION/KEEPING OF HERBS

There are various ways to keep herbs with drying and freezing being the most popular. Herbs can also be preserved in various mediums, e.g. vinegar, olive oil, butter, pesto, and sauce where their aromatic substances are maintained all year round. Freshly harvested herbs should be rinsed immediately under running water and then dried on cotton cloth before use.

FREEZING HERBS

Large quantities of fresh herbs are usually kept in freezers. Frozen herbs retain their aroma and ingredients for a wide variety of dishes. The fennel, basil and (spear)mint are frozen best than other herbs. Do not use these herbs for garnish, since they tend to soften and change in colour a little. It is better to chop them finely and place the pieces in ice-cube holders; fill cells with water and then freeze. There is no need to defrost the ice-cubes with the herbs; simply toss them in the pot and mix them with the food. Alternatively, chop the herbs finely or roughly and place them in plastic bags in small quantities. Herbs can also be preserved in butter or olive oil.

STORAGE CONTAINERS

The use of crumbled herbs is most convenient for meals and pastries. The same is true for powdered herbs. Mix 2-3 species of herbs of your choice and process them in a food mill. Seeds are usually kept whole, grated or shelled. Dried herbs, wild plants and seeds have a long shelf life, approximately a year. Keep glass jars and other airtight containers in a dark, cool place around the house. Use self-adhesive labels on jars with information about the herbs contained therein and their date of storage.

BASIC UTENSILS FOR CLEANING, CUTTING AND STORING HERBS / PLANTS

The following are the most basic utensils that should be available in your kitchen for cleaning, cutting and storing herbs/wild plants:

1) Colander
2) Plant drier
3) Mezza luna
4) Peeling knife
5) Slicing knife, pointed
6) Pair of kitchen gloves
7) Muslin cloth pieces (for bouquet garni)
8) Storage containers – labels

Use airtight containers to store herbs, flowers, and dried fruit, marmalade, fragrant olive oil and vinegar. The containers should be clean and dry. Transparent glass jars are best, since they allow us to ascertain, at any time, possible changes to their content. Herbs can be stored away in little bunches. However, a better way is to first crumble and place them in sachets.

Mezza luna:
A crescent-shaped, rocking knife is very useful for chopping large amounts of fresh herbs.

HERBS IN YOUR KITCHEN

Some people compare the significance of herbs for the kitchen with that of the sun for the earth!! Herbs are the life source for most food preparations. They provide not only taste, but also enhance the nutritional value of food. They are so versatile, that can virtually transform meals and pastries. King of the herbs for the Greek kitchen is the oregano, followed by the savory, (spear)mint and rosemary. For the Italian cuisine, the "royal family" consists of basil, sage and marjoram. The English love (spear)mint while the French prefer thyme and laurel. Saffron is the favourite herb for the Spanish and the Morocans.

The Greeks sprinkle oregano over fish, broiled meat, feta cheese and meat balls. The rosemary marries very well with fried fish and snails, while laurel with soups and legumes. Laurel is also used in the drying process of fruit (figs, grapes). Mint is used in recipes for pies and thyme for game. A lot of

wild plants applied as condiment in international cuisine are used for infusions by the Greeks. Such wild plants are: the sage, marjoram, thyme (with dittany), and chamomile.

Herbs are excellent for marinades and sauces, but also add excellent aroma to olive oil and vinegar. Some of the most popular herbs, e.g. the basil, oregano, fennel are indispensable for meat and fish dishes. For example, beef and veal dishes are best with rosemary, basil, marjoram or thyme. Also, chicken and turkey dishes combine very well with a wide range of herbs, e.g. thyme, oregano, saffron, and mint.

Pork marries perfectly with sage, laurel and rosemary, while lamb and goat dishes with oregano, rosemary, thyme, and mint sauce. Legumes, particularly the beans and lentils combine well with sage, laurel and oregano. Basil and mint are used in pasta dishes and mix well with yogurt, tomatoes and egg plants.

Herbs add a particular character to bread preparations, biscuits and sweet pies. It is best to use them fresh.

Liquors mixed with herbs also give a variety of palatable drinks; the same is true for refreshments with mint and yogurt. Sherbet is used to add fragrance to various pastries. The practice of mixing wines with herbs, particularly sage and saffron, has been known since antiquity.

Try to mix your favourite dried herbs to make your own blend. For example, put the following herbs in a mill and process them to powder: marjoram, thyme, basil, oregano or saffron, dill, parsley, and estragon. You can store them in little glass jars for future use.

A mouth-watering dish made from boiled wild roots and greens served with olive oil.

The culinary application of herbs requires prudence. On the one hand, herbs are indispensable for most meals, but excess use of them may ruin a particular dish for which you have spent a lot of money and effort. You should also know that fresh herbs offer a stronger fragrance than dried herbs. Therefore, be mindful of the quantities you use. In addition, not all herbs mix well with each other, particularly those with a strong fragrance. For example, sage is rather difficult to mix with other herbs.

TIPS FOR HERBS

- If you have no or little experience with herbs, then make use of them with moderation.
- Use one herb at a time, until you acquire the experience to combine them in dishes and pastries.
- For more information about herbs, look for the literature available in your area, or consult with an expert
- Herb blends are available at special stores where you can also get more information about herbal applications.

DRINKS

Herbal drinks, hot or cold, are very popular and easy to prepare. The rule is: one or one-half teaspoon of herb for a cup of water. When you use roots, rinds, or leaves, it is best to finely chop them first before use. The kitchen utensils required to make an infusion or tea should be made from enamel, porcelain or clay. Other kitchen utensils used for making herbal drinks are: strainer, kettle, cups with saucers. The time required to make a herbal infusion depends on the hardness of the particular herb. The following ways are used to prepare herbal teas and infusions:

1. Put as much water in a kettle as is required to make the amount of tea you desire. In a separate container place the quantity of herbs that corresponds to the number of servings you intend to produce. As soon as the water comes to the boil pour it over the herbs and cover the container for 10 minutes, then filter and serve.

2. Put the necessary amount of water and herbs in a container and boil for 2-3 minutes. Then turn off heat, but do not remove the container from the hot ring. Let the container rest on ring for 10 minutes, then filter the contents and serve.

3. Heat water (70-80oC) in a kettle, but do not let it come to the boil. Remove the kettle from the oven ring and pour the hot water over the herbs in a container. Cover the container for 7-8 minutes, filter and serve immediately.

4. Place as much of the herbs you require in a container and add water. Let the herbs soak for 3-4 hours, then strain and serve. Do not heat water or boil the herbs.

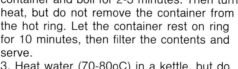
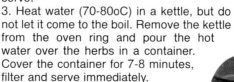
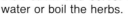

IT WAS WITH
BASIL AND MINT
THAT GOD BEDECKED THE WORLD

— ❧ ❧ ❧ —

Mentha piperita
Mentha spicata
Mentha silvestris
Mentha viridis
Mentha pulegium

This herb proliferates and interbreeds so easily that one can come across more that 20 different species with only insignificant differences among them, but all share the quality of emitting an intoxicating aroma.

◆ MYTHOLOGY – HISTORY

As Persephone was taking a stroll along the banks of river Acheron (in Greek and Roman mythology the river of woe), she stumbled upon her husband, Pluto, and his lover, young nymph Minthe.

In a fit of rage Persephone turned Minthe into a lowly plant with mauve tiny flowers, completely inconspicuous to human eyes. Pluto felt sorry for Minthe and endowed her with a divine fragrance. Since then, this lowly herb has been honoured profusely by gastrononers all over the world.

The ancien Greeks believed that mint could invigorate the mind and refresh blood. They also used it as a remedy for headaches. In fact, after nights of heavy drinking, ancient Greeks would place a wreath of mint on their heads to "exorcise" an impending hangover.

The Romans loved the smell of mint and had found ample culinary uses for it. They even scented their bathing water with this fine aromatic herb. Mint is also one of the ingredients for a sauce recipe by famous ancient Roman cook Atticius. This recipe consisted of the herb of grace (rue), mint, coriander, fennel, pepper, lovage, honey and some olive oil.

◆ POPULAR MEDICINE

Mint is considered an excellent tonic, antispasmodic and stomach comforter. It invigorates the function of liver and bile.

Steam baths in menthol, mint's volatile oil, are quite invigorating, antiseptic and disinfectant.

A teaspoon of honey in lukewarm fresh mint tea can check tummy aches/distension and stomach ulcers. It also checks the vomiting of women at gestation periods and motion sickness.

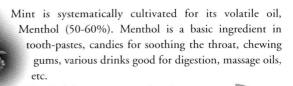

Mint is systematically cultivated for its volatile oil, Menthol (50-60%). Menthol is a basic ingredient in tooth-pastes, candies for soothing the throat, chewing gums, various drinks good for digestion, massage oils, etc.

Fliskuni

Menthol has strong antiseptic qualities and menthol compresses were used in the past to cure inflammatory skin diseases and herpes.

♦ CULTURE

It propagates quite easily and is officially known to produce 8 different species, however, experts believe that the mint family includes more than 30 species.

Differences among family members are identified in the shape and size of leaves, but more in fragrance and taste. Mint grows best in rich, moist soils. Mint is usually not grown from seed, but is easily propagated from roots or runners.

♦ HARVEST – PURCHASE – STORAGE

Mint is best to pick during early morning hours in Spring. If you need to dry it, first rinse it under cool, running water. Then place it in a cool, dark place. To keep it fresh for 3-4 days, store it in the refrigerator. Mint or spearmint in sealed packages maintains its aroma; never buy it in bulk.

♦ COOKING ♦

Mint gives a characteristic cool feeling and sweet fragrance. This makes it popular in kitchen applications. In ancient Greek cuisine mint was mainly used as ingredient in various sauces. The following extract from Athenaeus is quite characteristic: "[If] urchins are consumed in a sweet-sour sauce of vinegar and honey, with parsley and (spear)mint, they are sweet and tasty."

In modern Greek cuisine, freshly chopped mint is ideal for meatballs, eggplant salads, pumpkin pies and soft-cheese pies (kalitsounia).

In the Middle East, India, Africa and Persia (Iran) dried mint is used for spicing fish dishes and also added to milky drinks. Mint loses approximately 70% of its aroma when dried. In Europe, mint is also used in liqueurs, e.g., the Créme de Menthe, as well as in chocolates.
It is also used to prepare lamb sauces, added to fruit juice, orange and lemon water-ice.

THYME
THAT "KILLS" AND CURES

— ❦ ❦ ❦ —

Thymus vulgaris
Thymus serpyllum
Thymus pulegioides
Thymus capitatus
Thymus atticus
Thymus striatus

A symbol of power with invigorating qualities both for the mind and body. A small, compact shrublet with pink or whitish flowers grown on dry slopes and rocks in the Mediterranean. It adds colour to drab hills and attracts the bees like a magnet.

♦ MYTHOLOGY – HISTORY

Its ancient name "Thymus" comes from the Greek verb θύω meaning sacrifice. In the stock of incenses burnt on altars in ancient Greece were included fresh thyme leaves.

In ancient Greece the poor would consume an infusion made from thyme, honey and vinegar, while the elderly would drink large quantities of thyme tea to invigorate their mental faculties.

To increase their vigour and energy, Roman soldiers would bathe in water scented with thyme.

In 77 AD Pliny suggested thyme infusion compresses on the head as a cure for head aches. He also indicated thyme as an antidote for snake bites. In addition, the Romans would burn thyme outside their cottages to ward off scorpions.

During his expeditions, Alexander the Great would bathe in a thyme infusion in order to get rid of lice.

During the 16th century women would treat men with a soup sprinkled with dried thyme to increase their self-confidence. In the same age, people believed that sleeping on a pillow stuffed with thymus sprigs would cure melancholy.

♦ POPULAR MEDICINE

Cretans used to rub their gums with thyme to treat gingivitis. Today research has proved that gurgles with thyme tea is recommended for gingivitis, sore throats and acute cough. In

addition, thyme kills germs!! Its two basic volatile oils, thymole and carvacole, render thyme quite practical for antibacterial and antimicotic applications. Owing to these qualities thyme was combined in the past with soap for disinfecting the hands and surgical equipment before surgery operations in Europe.

Thyme infusions are soothing, aid digestion, comfort the stomach and relieve anxiety while they pep up the immune system. Bathing in thyme water is recommended for those suffering from rheumatism. Thyme cataplasms are excellent for treating wounds and itching from insect bites.

◆ CULTURE

There are more than 100 subspecies of thyme, many of which are for decorative applications. This plant grows best in light, well-drained soil. Propagate with cuttings, divisions, or by direct seeding. Thyme is an attractive edging plant or a spreading plant among and over rocks.

◆ HARVEST – PURCHASE – STORAGE

Cut leafy tops and flower clusters early in the morning and dry in bunches in a cool place away from the sun light. For culinary applications, crumble the dried thyme leaves and flowers and store them in airtight glass jars.
Always buy fresh thyme in bunches during the summer months. If you cannot find fresh thyme then choose medium-sized packages to get the most out of remaining freshness.

◆ COOKING ◆

Thyme is antiseptic, aromatic with a pungent taste, particularly when wild. Along with oregano, parsley, and marjoram, thyme is one of the main ingredients for "bouquet garni" that adds flavour to soups and sauces.

Greek cuisine makes good use of thyme's aromatic qualities in meatballs, stuffed vegetables, meat dishes, poultry and pies. In Cyprus there is a recipe for rabbit where the meat is placed on grill over entire roots of thyme.

In general, thyme fits well with meat (chicken, veal, rabbit) cooked in wine and tomato sauce. For the people of Marseilles thyme is considered an ideal seasoning even for fish!!

Check the recipe with aubergines (eggplants) sprinkled with finely chopped thyme.

To increase their mental capacities for better school performance, mothers in Lebanon serve their children with a slice of bread topped with a paste made from thyme and olive oil for breakfast.

SAGE
A HERB FOR IMMORTALS

— ❧ ❧ ❧ —

Salvia officinalis
Salvia purpurascens
Salvia sclarea
Salvia pomifera
Salvia verbenacana
Salvia triloba

This grey-green with hairy leaves and terminal heads of violet flowers plant grows in abundance on the hills and mountains of Crete. It has aroused considerable interest among botanists and physicians owing to its significant therapeutic qualities.

This explains its Latin name "Salvia" from the Latin root *salvare* meaning to save.

♦ MYTHOLOGY – HISTORY

For centuries now the Chinese have developed a unique system of popular medicine based on herbs. Sage for them was so valuable that they traded it with triple the amount of the best quality of the best quality of tea they imported during the Middle Ages.

Ancient Greek botanists and physicians, for example Theofrastus Dioscurides and Hippocrates, were familiar with the therapeutic qualities and applications of sage. Dioscurides reports sage as balsam for sore eyes and effective medicine for hemorrhage. In antiquity sage infusions were believed to restore memory and increase life expectancy.

For the Romans sage was a divine plant and used as an antidote even for snake bites.

Charlemagne encouraged its systematic cultivation in Germany. During the Middle Ages, sage was used extensively against cholera, high fever and epilepsy. When plague broke out in Toulouze in 1690, thieves would wash themselves thoroughly with sage and rosemary extract to protect themselves from deadly infections while looting the dead lying on streets. This is explained by the fact that along with the disinfectant qualities of rosemary, the phenolic acids in the leaves of sage offered extra antiseptic and antibacterial protection.

♦ POPULAR MEDICINE

In Greece, and the entire Balkan region in general, sage oil was used extensively as popular medicine against headaches, mouth ulcers, tonsilitis, also for massaging the abdominal area to relieve pain. Sage infusions

are recommended for relieving colds, sore throat and the flu. It aids digestions and restores peptic functions. In addition, the oil of Salvia sclarea is used in aromatherapy applications.

◆ HARVEST – PURCHASE – STORAGE

For best results harvest sage from end of May to end of June, when efflorescence is at its peak. There are two sage varieties, the broad-leaved and the inrolled at the edges. The former is mild in taste and indicated for culinary uses.

Collect the broad-leaved plant early in the morning and dry it in a cool and dark place, so that it retains its aroma. Store in airtight jars. Always buy sage in bunches during the summer months when it is fresh.

Dried Sage

◆ CULTURE

An annual with herbaceous stems plant that grows mainly in mild and hot climates. Approximately 250 subspecies have been recorded around the world, 20 of which are found in Greece. Broad-leaved sage is easy to grow from seeds, particularly during Spring. Sage transplanted to large flower pots or directly to soil can grow faster in sunny places.

◆ COOKING ◆

Sage is very popular with the Italian cuisine. It offers a slightly bitter and pungent taste and goes well with pork, duck, sausage and bacon. The effect is that it reduces the taste of fat. Sage also marries well with fried rabbit, shrimps and fish rich in fat, e.g. eels.

On Crete sage is also used in the process of smoking sausages because it imparts its aroma to the meat. In addition, the traditional hard bread of Crete tastes better if you insert twigs of sage in the wood-fired oven. There is a traditional recipe for fried pork liver where sage substitutes rosemary.

Fry sage leaves until they become crispy, then dip them in porridge. They taste excellent.

Fresh sage leaves are usually inserted into legumes packs to ward off bugs.

LAUREL
DEDICATED TO APOLLO

— ❧ ❧ ❧ —

Laurus nobilis

A delicate bushy tree with nice, dark green leatherly leaves

and impressive yellowish flowers.

The root *laur* in Laurus is either Celtic meaning green or

Latin meaning praise or honour.

♦ MYTHOLOGY – HISTORY

Apollo fell in love with the daughter of river-god Ladonas, Dafne, an extremely beautiful maiden, but quite independent, even a wild creature. When Apollo chased her to express his love for her, she took refuge with goddess Gea (Earth) who transformed her into a slender tree, the laurel tree.

The myth goes on with Apollo slaying the dragon Python at the banks of a river; then Apollo bathed in the waters of this river, cut laurel sprigs from its banks and marched triumphant into the town of Delphi crowned with laurel leaves. Since then the laurel became a symbol of purification, victory, glory and honour. The laurel plant was also sacred to physician Asclepius.

♦ POPULAR MEDICINE

The women of Crete would expose to direct sunlight a vase of green olive oil with laurel berries. This oil was used as hair tonic, for massaging the limbs suffering from rheumatism or for muscle fractures. Farmers would also sprinkle their stock with laurel-water to keep away parasites. In addition, the powder from dried laurel leaves is good for stopping hemorrhage from the nose.

Furthermore, laurel tea aids stomach function and digestion.

◆ HARVEST – PURCHASE – STORAGE

The laurel leaves lose their colour and aroma during the process of drying. In this case, also, we should be aware of the golden rule that applies to drying herbs: "keep them away from the sun!". Laurel leaves are usually kept in sachets or jars that are tightly sealed. When purchasing laurel leaves choose from airtight packages.

◆ CULTURE

Laurel is an evergreen shrub which requires rich soil to grow, ample sunlight and protection from the wind. You can grow it from seeds or, even better, buy cuttings and transplant it during the Spring.

◆ COOKING ◆

In the traditional Greek and Cretan cuisine, laurel leaves were used to add aroma to dried figs and raisins, as well as to keep bugs away. Laurel leaves are added to lentil soups, veal or rabbit stews and also used for the making of traditional yeast ("kounenos") for special bread made from chickpea flour.

Laurel is part of the bouquet garni of aromatic herbs used to add flavour to various soups, rice dishes, and grilled meat. You can also find it in pork and/or veal jellies.

When laurel leaves are allowed to soak in lukewarm milk the latter takes a pleasant sweet taste and aroma. Laurel is also used in puddings and milk pies. Make moderate use of laurel leaves particularly when fresh. This plant's aroma and taste is quite strong.

ROSEMARY

A SYMBOL OF BEAUTY THAT ALSO DRIVES EVIL SPIRITS AWAY

— ❧ ❧ ❧ —

Rosmarinus officinalis

An elixir of youth, a symbol of beauty and well-being, a gift from goddess Venus to the people. This herb is an evergreen decorative shrub in the labiatae (mint) family with significant gastronomic and other applications by the peoples of the Mediterranean.

◆ MYTHOLOGY – HISTORY

Rosemary was used as incense in antiquity and burnt on shrines during sacrificial rites to propitiate the gods.

Botanist Alpini discovered whole twigs of rosemary inside an Egyptian mummy. This was probably either for practical reasons (embalming) or a ritual requirement. This aromatic plant was also used as herbs of remembrance and was added to wedding bouquets and carried to funeral processions. The rosemary was also used as a preservative.

In the Middle Ages the popular belief was that rosemary grew spontaneously in the yards of the righteous, that it brought good luck and

drove evil spirits and witches away. In addition, rosemary boosts memory. This belief is confirmed by a practice of the ancient Greeks who used to crown themselves with a rosemary wreath in periods of intensive study.

In a botanological paper of 1526 AD discovered on Crete, we read: "Rosemary is for curing the weakness of mind and cold. Immerse rosemary leaves in wine, seal the container and store in a warm place". In another paper dating from the Middle Ages we get the following recipe: "If you feel weak, boil rosemary leaves in clear water and then wash your face which it will shine . . . inhale the vapour and you will feel young."

◆ POPULAR MEDICINE

Rosemary tea was used extensively for soothing headaches. Volatile oils obtained from rosemary were also used to cure migraines. Rosemary is considered ideal for treating the head against hair-loss and is an ingredient for hair lotions.

It offers significant antibacterial qualities and was used as antiseptic and disinfectant in French hospitals in the beginning of 20th century.

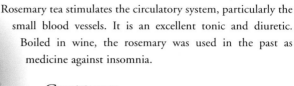

Rosemary tea stimulates the circulatory system, particularly the small blood vessels. It is an excellent tonic and diuretic. Boiled in wine, the rosemary was used in the past as medicine against insomnia.

Dried rosemary

◆ CULTURE

Rosemary is an evergreen bushy shrub up to 1 ½ m high with lance-shaped leaves, and mauve-blue (occasionally white) flowers. It grows best in sunny regions, even near the coastlines (hence its Latin name "Rosemarinus"), particularly around the Mediterranean. It can be cultivated on any kind of soil, even rocky, while it propagates by cuttings from a larger plant. Before transplanting, place seedlings in water for 5-6 days. It flowers in March to June.

◆ HARVEST – PURCHASE – STORAGE

Snip the tender foliage early in the morning or late noon all year round. Place leaves on cotton cloth and dry in a cool and dark place. Store dried rosemary leaves in airtight jars. Excellent quality rosemary can be found in packages and is ideal for cooking.

◆ COOKING ◆

Rosemary is a favourite ingredient for the Mediterranean cuisine. It is used to add flavour and colour to vegetable oils, vinegar and cooking salt. It goes well with veal, lamb, game and poultry. Rosemary is also used as a preservative. A quite popular culinary application is the "savoro" dish, fried fish, which can be kept outside the fridge for 5-6 days during the winter. Rosemary is a must for the popular on Crete recipe of fried snails in olive oil.
In Italy rosemary is used in spaghetti sauces, bread, pizza and pastries!! Fresh rosemary offers a better taste and aroma. High ranking chefs place lamb legs on a bed of fresh rosemary leaves for better taste.

SAFFRON CROCUS
THE HERB OF THE SUN

— ❧ ❧ ❧ —

Crocus sativus

A Minoan wall-painting kept in the archaeological Museum of Heraklion depicts an ape picking crocus flowers and offering them to a Minoan goddess.

◆ MYTHOLOGY – HISTORY

According to mythology, Crocus was a real person and friend to god Hermes (Mercury). He was fatally wounded while throwing the disc in a competition with the god. A small flower with shiny stamens sprang from his blood that spilled on the earth.

The saffron plant was probably known to the Minoans and grown by them in specially designed "crocus-gardens", particularly for its deep-purple pistils and orange red stigmas that were used in cooking and the art of dyeing. The crocus is possibly a native of ancient Mesopotamia but has also naturalized elsewhere in the Mediterranean.

Strabo and Dioscurides make numerous references to this plant and its medicinal, culinary, and dyeing applications. Theophrastus speaks of the "crocinus myrrh" taken from the same plant and was considered of high economic value as early as 1600 BC. Crocus flowers were also spread in public halls, courtesans' areas, public baths and theatres.

The Mauritans of Spain were the first to practice systematic cultivation of saffron. Large quantities of saffron were exported from Spain to Persia (Iran), Asia Minor and China. During that time saffron was not popular in Europe.

◆ POPULAR MEDICINE

Owing to its aphrodisiac qualities saffron was associated, particularly in ancient times, with the courtesans. It is rich in vitamin B2, an excellent tonic and tummy sedative. It sooths and detoxifies the liver.

The saffron crocus was associated with child bearing in India, China, Casmir and Persia, although it is likely that in large quantities it may be implicated for abortion. From ancient Greek mythology we learn that Gaea, the mother of Zeus, spread crocus flowers on her son's nuptial bed to expedite the child-bearing of goddess Hera. Dioscurides recommends this plant for ailments of the uterus and Galen for inflammation of the eyes.

Currently, it is believed that systematic consumption of the saffron crocus in small quantities may delay the effects of aging and invigorate the brain. This explains the popular use of the plant in India during spiritual practices.

◆ CULTURE

Today the saffron crocus is cultivated in northern Greece, particularly in Kozani, Spain, Sicily, Iran and Casmir.

It grows spontaneously in barren and uncultivated fields in the Cyclades insular complex, mainly at Astypalaea, Syros, Tenos, Myconos and Delos. Excellent quality saffron is cultivated in the Crocus area of Kozani where more than 10 tons of this plant are produced every year. The entire production is exported to the Middle East, England, Japan and the USA. Also, top quality saffron is produced in Casmir.

Dried crocus stamens

◆ HARVEST – PURCHASE – STORAGE

Crocus harvest is a tedious task since all three orange-red stigmas are picked individually from each fresh flower. The stigmas are laid on trays and dried in open wood fire. It has been estimated that 75,000 flowers yield approximately 450 grams of aromatic saffron. This precious gift of nature is available in the market at packages of $1/4$ gram or in small glass jars. Store packages in a cool place to prevent any changes to saffron's aroma and taste. If you buy the stamens, pick those of intense yellow or red colour and make sure that they are genuine since substitutes, like "kourkoumas" are also available in the market. You would be better off with genuine saffron since 1-2 stamens suffice for spicing your dishes with this unique seasoning.

◆ COOKING ◆

Saffron is used extensively in bread-making around the Mediterranean, in Scandinavia and the Balkan region. It is the main ingredient in the French bouillabaisse, adds a distinctive red colour to Spanish Paella and to scores of rice and meat dishes of the Indian and Persian cuisine. In India saffron is added to wedding meals and pastries. This excellent spice was very popular on Crete up to the 17th century, however its use is currently restricted to Easter and religious festivities for bread preparations, crisp/hard bread making, pastries and pastas in the isles of Astypalaea, Santorini, Folegandros, and Anafi. For culinary applications, make sure you dilute saffron in water and then add it to food, otherwise you will get a bitter tasting dish.

BASIL

THE ROYALTY AMONGST
THE HERB FAMILY

— ❧ ❧ ❧ —

Ocimum basilicum

This is a refreshing, aromatic and sublime herb with over five hundred species identified around the world. It won a kingly position in gardens and kitchens and is used for medicinal purposes in India.

♦ MYTHOLOGY – HISTORY

The Hindi name for basil is Tulsi; a plant dedicated to a Hindu nymph by the same name who, like Dafne, was transformed to a bush in order to escape an amorous god of the Far East. Today basil is the sacred plant of Vishnu in India.

Four thousand years ago basil spread from India to other parts of the world, Africa and Egypt, and much later (16th c. AD) to Greece. The natives of W. Africa used basil as antifebrile medicine; the Egyptians mixed basil with myrrh during the process of embalment.

For the Romans basil took a more romantic turn; however, Apicius was more practical and left us with a recipe – "Peas in basil sauce". In Italy and Crete basil is a symbol of love, while a man accepting a sprig of basil from a young woman in these regions was considered officially engaged to this woman.

Basil is considered sacred in the Ortho-dox Church. It is said to have grown in the location where St. Helen discovered the Holly Cross.

♦ POPULAR MEDICINE

Dioscurides recommended basil against dysuria. Mashed basil leaves were traditionally used as an antidote to mosquito and snake bites. Basil tea is good for digestion and sooths the intestines. Basil extracts act against thrush and herpes of the mouth. It is also good for migraines, headaches and motion sickness and pregnancy nausea. Following childbirth, women chew basil leaves to increase their production of milk. Dried basil leaves are recommended for chronic rhinitis and sinusitis. Basil is also used in aromatherapy.

♦ CULTURE

Basil, a tender annual, grows in a bush to about two feet tall. Plant basil in a sunny location in a well-drained, fairly rich soil. Basil is easily grown from seeds. In warm areas, it can be directly seeded into the garden. Often grown into the garden as a companion plant to tomatoes; it repels white flies and gnats. Basil in a variety of colours, size and aromas is easily grown in gardens and pots. The "athanatos", meaning immortal, variety grows in Greece and stays green even in winter.

♦ HARVEST – PURCHASE – STORAGE

To enjoy basil to the maximum, snip fresh leaves and add them to meals. If you need to dry the leaves, collect them early in the morning or at dusk, when the plant is not at blossom; otherwise the aroma will be lost. Place basil leaves on a cotton cloth and dry them in a cool and dark place. Basil leaves can be maintained fresh up to 4-5 months when kept in olive oil. Similarly, you can boil the leaves and keep them fresh in the freezer.

In the market you can find fresh basil leaves in packages and jars. Keep them away from the sun.

♦ COOKING ♦

Basil is the main ingredient in "pesto a la Genoveze", an Italian sauce for spaghetti. The ingredients of this sauce are: fresh basil leaves, pine seeds, garlic and parmesan cheese. Basil is the most favourite herb for the Italian cuisine and combines with fresh vegetables (tomatoes, eggplants, and courgettes). Basil is also found in the Verde sauce that marries well with pasta, boiled potatoes and fresh beans.

Basil also combines well with fresh tomatoes, mozzarella or other soft cheese, e.g. sweet and sour cheese, and good quality vinegar.

FENNEL

— ?❧ ?❧ ?❧ —

Foeniculum vulgare

The fennel has been popular since ancient times, particularly in ancient Egypt, Greece and Rome. Currently, it occupies a prominent place among the aromatic herbs of the international cuisine.

◆ CULTURE

The fennel is fairly easy to cultivate either by seeds or bulbs from the wild fennel species. Transplantation should take place in Autumn. Sow in mild and moist soil. Harvesting starts in January.

◆ MYTHOLOGY – HISTORY

For ancient Greeks fennel was a symbol of success and its name probably derives from "Marathonas", a location near Athens where ancient Greeks defeated the Persians in 490 B.C. Pliny believed that snakes ate fennel to shed their skins easily. The Hindus and the Chinese considered fennel a strong antidote against snake and scorpion bites. King Charlemagne believed that fennel warded off evil spirits and used it to block the key-holes of his bedroom doors to keep the evil away.

◆ HARVEST – PURCHASE – STORAGE

Wild fennel grows in uncultivated plots, crevises, and river banks, and is harvested from January to April. In May and June fennel leaves loose their softness and develop larvae. Seeds may be collected in summer.

If you intend to purchase fennel from your local market, make sure that the fennel you choose is tender. Chop fennel sprigs finely and place them on a cotton cloth to dry in a cool and dark place. Subsequently, you place the pieces in glass jars and store them away in a dry place. Soak fresh fennel leaves and roughly chopped roots in warm water before storing them in the freezer.

◆ POPULAR MEDICINE

Fennel seeds were used by the women of Crete in the past to make a strong tea which they mixed with yogurt and honey to make a facial beauty mask that was believed to remove wrinkles.

In antiquity Hippocrates and Discourides believed that fennel facilitated the flow of mothers' milk. Since then, the fennel has been very popular with breastfeeding women around the Mediterranean.

Mixed with sage, the fennel was also used to relieve colic and renal pain. Both its seeds and root are good for digestion. This information was known to the people of the Middle Ages.

The fennel is also used as diuretic while the tea from its seeds is believed to cleanse the kidneys from little stones and detoxify the liver.

◆ COOKING ◆

The fennel enjoys wide culinary applications on Crete and mainland Greece. You can find it in cottage pies, mixed with octopus, cuttlefish, fish, snails, while it also marries well with legumes (e.g. black-eyed beans, broadbeans) and fresh vegetables (fresh beans and artichokes).

If you want to add aroma to fatty fish, cook the fish on grill under a layer of fresh fennel sprigs. Use the fennel seeds to add fragrance to green olives or make bread.

ROCKET
THE HOT DIVA OF THE MEDITERRANEAN

— ❧ ❧ ❧ —

Eruca sativa

This mustard-like plant with pale yellow or whitish petals is cultivated as a salad plant. The plant part used are the seeds, 1 to 2 mm in diameter. Although called "white mustard", the seeds are yellow to light brown. Some people believe that the seeds make an excellent salad, others, however, detest their pungent taste. Nevertheless, the plant has captured the imagination of Italian, Greek and American gourmets.

fresh and whole. Keep the bunches of rocket in the fridge for about 3-4 days.

♦ MYTHOLOGY – HISTORY

Its Latin name derives from the Roman verb *urere* meaning "to burn" and refers to its pungent taste. Agapios Monachos the Cretan (15th c. A.D.) reports: "The rocket, cress, and celery are hot and good for digestion. They tempt the flesh and cause headaches, [therefore] it is best to consume them with such cold greens as purslane, lettuce, and chicory…"

♦ POPULAR MEDICINE

Consumed raw, rocket stimulates the appetite.

♦ HARVEST – PURCHASE – STORAGE

Pick the fresh leaves before the plant blossoms to get the most out of their pungent taste. Always buy little bunches where the leaves are

♦ CULTURE

The rocket flourishes mainly in hot climates, mainly in the Mediterranean, where 3-4 species have been recorded. The plant is easily cultivated from seeds which should be planted at some distance. Water regularly. For better results sow the seeds during the winter. If you sow in sunny locations, harvesting can take place in 4-5 weeks. Transplanting the rocket is not recommended. All three species can be found in the market.

♦ COOKING ♦

The fresh piquant rocket leaves are used in Italy with a touch of vinegar, olive oil for meat or pasta stuffing. Mixing rocket leaves with lettuce, purslane, tomatoes, dill and fresh broad beans or onions makes an excellent salad.

NETTLE

PROTECTS FROM
ANNUAL AILMENTS (HESIOD)

— ❧ ❧ ❧ —

Urtica urens
Urtica dioica

It took fourteen centuries for people to realise that Hesiode's remark about nettles were no exaggeration. This herbaceous plant with stinging hairs on leaves has excellent nutritional and medicinal qualities.

♦ MYTHOLOGY – HISTORY

The Urtica genus derives its name from the Latin verb *uro*, to burn, referring to the burning sensation one feels from the effects of fluid (poison) contained in the stinging hairs with which the leaves are so well armed. On their expeditions in cold climates, Roman soldiers rubbed themselves with nettle leaves to produce a burning heat sensation on their bodies. The ancient Greeks supplemented their meals with nettle dishes so much that Aristopanes, the comic dramatist, suggested to his fellow citizens to grow nettles in their gardens.

Apicius (25 AD) recommended the following a few centuries ago: "When the sun is in Aries, snip female nettles and use them as medicine".

Following this, Apicius provides a recipe for a nettle omelette with good quality olive oil and a lot of pepper.

Petrinius, writer in the age of Nero, recommended flogging ("Urtication") the navel, kidneys and bottom to those men who wanted to revive their sexuality. Urtication was an old remedy for chronic rheumatism and loss of muscular power.

♦ POPULAR MEDICINE

The nettle is one of the most precious gifts of nature to people. It is an excellent arrester of bleeding (haemostasis), and stimulates the circulation of blood; it is also a remedy for diabetes and, because it is rich in vitamins A and C, offers protection against scurvy. Nettle cataplasms are used against eczema and nose bleeding. The nettles are also rich in Carotene B which prevents the development of free radicals. The homeopathic tincture, Urtica, is frequently administered successfully for rheumatic gout, also for nettlerash and chickenpox, and externally for bruises. The nettle is also used in the preparation of a lotion and soap for hair conditioning.

◆ HARVEST – PURCHASE – STORAGE

Nettles are found almost anywhere in the country side, in your unattended garden, in parks, even on road sides. Actually, the nettle is spread world-wide with approximately 500 species mainly tropical. The analysis of the fresh nettle shows the presence of formic acid, mucilage, mineral salts, ammonia, carbonic acid and water. It is because of the formic acid that nettle stings cause irritation and inflammation. Use plastic gloves to pick and clean nettles, or boil them for 15 minutes to neutralize irritating agents. Nettles are harvested from December to April, before they blossom. You can find them in the market mixed with other greens. Soak them in boiled water, pack and store them in the freezer to keep them fresh. Dry them in a cool place, away from the sun. Store them in jars.

◆ CULTURE

There is no systematic cultivation, but if you decide to keep those found in your garden, water them regularly if you need them fresh during the winter time.

◆ COOKING ◆

They offer an intense grass-like taste and can be used for soups and pies in combination with other greens (spinach, sorrel, onions, and spices). A quite palatable nettle-rice dish is made in Macedonia, while in Italy nettles are cooked with risotto and ample pecorino cheese. Fried nettles and eggs with butter is another excellent dish. Nettles are quite popular greens and find numerous culinary applications in Epirus, Macedonia and Thrace.

PURSLANE
AS VALUABLE AS OLIVE OIL

— ᘰ ᘰ ᘰ —

Portulaca oleracea

In the Mediterranean, when in the heart of the summer all wild greens are dry and yellowish-brown in colour and thistles in blossom, a small plant with fleshy, reddish stems and thick succulent leaves is also in blossom. You can find it in gardens, under tomato, red pepper and marrow beds.

◆ MYTHOLOGY – HISTORY

It is not known when this plant first naturalized in the Mediterranean. However, it was known to ancient Greeks since we have more than a dozen references in our hands today from Dioscurides, Galenus (Galen), and Pliny. The latter says that purslane can be used as "charm against all evil"
Agapios Monachos the Cretan (15th c. AD) wrote, "It is cold and astringent. The cultivated purslane is better than the wild; it stops stomach burning and sooths the intestines…" When consumed with food of high acidity, it can not be digested easily. It combines best with basil, garlic, cress, and piquant greens."

◆ POPULAR MEDICINE

Dioscurides used purslane for ailments of the stomach and eyes. Galinus speaks of the excellent medicinal properties of purslane's juice. Currently, purslane is used in salads and rarely as medicine. In spite of this, recent medical research in Europe and the USA proved that the purslane is rich in linoleic acid which is cardiotonic.

◆ HARVEST – PURCHASE – STORAGE

Collect the tender purslane leaves and sprigs from locations that are in shade and with ample moisture. You can also find this plant in bunches in Mediterranean fruit markets. Keep refrigerated for 3-4 days.

◆ CULTURE

Purslane grows in fields, flower pots and gardens all over Greece, Spain, Italy, Egypt, Morocco, Turkey, and India. It also grows from seeds. Sow from April to May and you will be able to collect three weeks later.

◆ COOKING ◆

Chop finely and mix with tomatoes, cucumbers, rocket, onion and feta cheese for a very tasty salad. Purslane and yogurt is a refreshing salad popular in Turkey. A tasty dish is also chicken with fresh courgettes in tomato sauce mixed with purslane.

ASPARAGUS
THE SLENDER BODY OF PERIGOUN

— ଏ ଏ ଏ —

Asparagus officinalis
Asparagus acutifolius

This woody-stemmed plant offers a pleasant, sweet taste and marries well with meat and fish dishes. Its tender stalks are used for salads and soups. The asparagus is not only an excellent delicacy, but also good for health.

♦ MYTHOLOGY – HISTORY

It was dusk and the waters of the Corinth Isthmus were at a stand-still while god Poseidon was resting in his deep blue kingdom of the sea. It was also Spring, a time for offerings to the goddess of earth Demeter. Suddenly, the air filled the human ears with a horrible cry . It was from Perigoun, the daughter of notorious bandit Zine. She was being chased by Theseus who wanted to make her his bride. Desperate Perigun pleaded with the gods for a safe place to hide. At that time her dress was caught in the spikes of a bush and the girl turned into a tender asparagus shoot. Since then the plant was dedicated to goddess Aphrodite (Venus) and the people of Viotoia adopted the custom of dressing the brides-to-be with branches of wild asparagus.
Pliny reports of asparagus as a medicinal plant.

♦ POPULAR MEDICINE

Ancient food expert Atheneus believed that the asparagus cures all bowel ailments. Agapios Monachos the Cretan (15th c.) ascribed aphrodisiac qualities to asparagus and considered the same as medicine for stomach complaints. The asparagus is rich in magnesium, phosphorus, vitamins C and E, folic acid and carotene. The asparagus is also diuretic and laxative, particularly its juice. It contains a nitrogenous substance, the Asparagine, which is necessary for the production and regeneration of the body cells.

♦ HARVEST – PURCHASE – STORAGE

In the Mediterranean basin the wild asparagus is harvested early in Spring. It grows in olive groves, under oak trees, pines and planes. Wild asparagus are rarely found in the market and prices are very high. White, mauve and green asparagus species are also available in the market from early Spring to June. Asparagus is sold in bunches of ½ kilo and can be kept in the fridge for 4-5 day wrapped in a wet cloth.

♦ CULTURE

Sow seeds in seed-plots from March to April and transplant to fertile soil a year later. Roots are also available in the market.

♦ COOKING ♦

In Greece asparagus is cooked in casseroles and pots or added to omelets. Thick spears are cooked in butter and for well with sauces and meat. Thick creamy soups, pies and risotto are also produced from cultivated asparagus.
White asparagus, usually canned, is less tasty. On the other hand, the green asparagus is a fine delicacy.

BORAGE
A HERB FOR THE MELANCHOLY

— ❧ ❧ ❧ —

Borago officinalis

This is a lovely herb with purple anthers and hairy foliage. For centuries people believed that this herb offers significant medicinal value, particularly to people suffering from melancholy!

♦ MYTHOLOGY – HISTORY

According to mythology, it was borage that caused fair Helen to abandon her lawfully wedded husband, Menelaus, which subsequently resulted in the Trojan War. It is said that when Helen tasted the tops of the borage herb she absconded with Paris to Troy.

Pliny reports that borage brings joy and happiness to people who cultivate it or are near it. An old text dating from 15 c.A.D. reports the following, "This herb is beneficial to all people, healthy or ailing alike. When consumed regularly, it has a beneficial effect on character. Two famous botanists of 16th c., John Gerard and John Evelyn, are of the same opinion, "The virtues of borage are quite known; it invigorates the hypochondriacs and refreshes the mind of those studying hard". In the Middle Ages Albert the Great attributed to borage revitalizing qualities.

♦ POPULAR MEDICINE

Borage tea was used for revitalization of the mind, mainly by those steeped in intensive mental labour or those suffering from depression. Recent research confirmed that this herb, in addition to the fact that it is rich in potassium and calcium, also contains γ-linolenic acid which offers protection from various diseases such as cancer and heart ailments. It stimulates the suprarenal cortex and acts as tonic and diuretic. From the seeds and leaves of borage we obtain a certain emulsion that can be used for mouth washes.

◆ HARVEST – PURCHASE – STORAGE

Before any culinary application, collect the tender borage leaves early in winter. The flowers can be collected any time of the day. If you need to use the leaves, flowers or seeds for tea, collect them early in the morning. To dry borage leaves, flowers and seeds, place them on a used newspaper or other absorbent paper and place then in a dark, cool place. Rig up a string or wire to hang the entire plant upside down in a shady place and let it dry.

You will rarely find borage in the market, however, the seeds are easily found. Fresh leaves and flowers can be maintained in the fridge for 4-5 days sealed in a plastic bag.

◆ CULTURE

You can easily grow borage from seeds in your garden or in flower pots. Sow from October to December in moderately moist soil.

◆ COOKING ◆

Borage is a culinary herb mostly popular in Central Europe. Cooks in the Elizabethan era would add the purple borage flowers in their salads for colour and aroma. The same is currently true in other parts of the world: the USA, northern Europe and Australia.

Borage's taste is rather weak and very similar to fresh cucumber. This marries well with salads, various greens, chicory, or lettuce. Borage is frequently used to flavour wines or vinegar. In Turkey the leaves are usually stuffed with rice and/or minced meat.

POPPY
THE FLOWER
OF GODDESS DEMETER

— ❧ ❧ ❧ —

Papaver ghoeas

Poppies and their minute seeds are associated with a range of fertility rites and rituals, and medicinal practices in Greece and the broader Mediterranean region.

◆ MYTHOLOGY – HISTORY

According to Greek mythology, when Demeter found out that the god of Hades had kidnapped her daughter Persephone, she took a potent drink, the "afioni", made from a variety of poppy flowers, to numb her emotional pain. When the goddess finally came round, she descended the prairies and valleys to fertilize the land and return to people the rich yield of the land. In the Archaeological Museum of Heraklion there is a statuette of the Late Minoan era featuring two poppy capsules on its head. These capsules probably signify health and fertility. Athenaeus of antiquity reports that poppy seeds were used to make fine quality bread.

◆ POPULAR MEDICINE

We know that ancient physicians used poppy seeds and capsules for their narcotic properties. The poppy flower probably originates from West Asia, but has been grown in Europe since the Neolithic era. It is probably one of the earliest plants cultivated by man. The species named "Meekoon the somniferum" was probably exported from Egypt to Greece. Poppy the papaver, the commonest cornfield poppy, is usually found in wasteland but sunny places, fields and among the cornfields. It contains a slightly narcotic substance which is won from its petals and was once administered as sedative to children of very young age. In addition, the infusions from the fruits are good for coughs. Today an extract from poppy flowers gives an effective syrup for cough.

Poppy heads

◆ HARVEST– PURCHASE – STORAGE

The young, hairy and lance-shaped leaves of the poppy are collected late in winter and just before they blossom (April – May). Poppy flowers in bunches and mixed with fennel and sorrel are usually available in Greek fruit markets. Poppy seeds are available in special stores. You can keep fresh poppy leaves in the fridge for up to 6 days and slightly cooked in the freezer. The seeds may change fast, so it is better to keep them in the fridge or into a cool place for a few days. Always buy seeds in small quantities.

◆ CULTURE

More than ten species of poppies have been recorded in Greece. Ornamental varieties are usually cultivated from bulbs planted early in spring.

◆ COOKING ◆

Owing to their fragrance, fresh poppy leaves found ample culinary applications, e.g. they were used for making pies stuffed with a blend of other herbs. Poppy leaves fits well with spinach, leek, sorrel and fennel. The poppy seeds are used to make tasty bread, crackers and cakes.

OREGANO
AT THE TOP OF THE
MEDITERRANEAN CUISINE

— 🐦 🐦 🐦 —

Origanum Vulgare

It grows in wasteland areas and sunny places in the Mediterranean and flowers in the heart of the summer. It features round leaves and minute white flowers that attract bees like magnets.

◆ MYTHOLOGY – HISTORY

The Greek name *origanon* might well contain the terms *óros* ("mountain") and *ganos* "mountain splendour"). Dioscurides recommended this herb to those who had lost their appetite.

◆ POPULAR MEDICINE

The ancient Greeks made tea from oregano to cure the spasms of the abdomen and as an antidote to food poisoning. Oregano concoctions are antiseptic, sligh-

tly bitter in taste and act against diarrhea. In Crete fried in olive oil oregano leaves were used to produce an ointment for curing stiffness of the back and hips. In the past oregano and olive oil was also used for toothaches.

◆ HARVEST – PURCHASE – STORAGE

This herbaceous plant is found wild mainly in

stony and sunny places in the Mediterranean. Collect the sprigs and flowers together early in the summer, from May to July (depending on the location). In Greece you can find dried oregano in bunches or crumbled in jars or plastic bags.

If you buy oregano in bunches, it is better to wrap it in a thin kitchen film and hang it upside down on a string to keep the aroma from dissipating. In general, the aroma and colour of herbs is usually maintained by drying herbs in a cool, dark place. Place a few oregano spring between your palms and rub them to crumbs. Store crumbs in jars for later use.

Dried oregano leaves can be maintained for years if stored in airtight jars and kept away from the sun. Fresh oregano leaves are stored in the freezer.

♦ CULTURE

Carefully pluck oregano plants from the roots in winter or early spring and transplant to pots and later to soil. Transplanted seedlings will grow into robust plants during the second year. Not much water is required.

♦ COOKING ♦

Oregano is a sine qua non for the Greek and the Mediterranean cuisine. Its piquant taste marries well with virgin olive oil and lemon for sauce. A lot of dishes in Crete and Greece are served with or cooked in this sauce, e.g. goat's meat, potatoes, liver, fish, even boiled courgettes. In many islands of the Dodekanense and Cycaldes, oregano is sprinkled over grilled fish to add flavour. The same is also true for cottage ("Horiatiki") salad and feta cheese. Oregano also fits well with pizzas and bread that are baked with cumin, tomatoes and olive oil. It is also used to add flavour to olive oil, vinegar and black olives.

MALLOW
TO EASE DIGESTION
AND FREE THE SPIRIT

— 🍵 🍵 🍵 —

Malva silvestris
Malva moschata
Malva cretica

The fact that this plant remains neglected during our century is quite surprising, despite its popularity in previous centuries. The mallow was cultivated as an edible plant by the ancient Greeks and Romans, even by the Byzantines.

Today it is used mainly for infusions and tea.

◆ MYTHOLOGY – HISTORY

Hesiod reports of the medicinal qualities of mallow that grew in Attica. He considered this plant as food for the poor, but also noted its botanological significance and gastronomic applications. The nutritional value of mallow was extolled by Cicero, Horace and Marialis . In addition, Horace said that his diet consisted exclusively of olives, chicory and mallow. For the Romans mallow was an excellent table delicacy while Apicius left us with a recipe where fish was served with a piquant sauce with mallow as its main ingredient. For the Byzantines the mallow was a wild vegetable of two distinct types.

◆ POPULAR MEDICINE

Centuries ago Difilos from the isle of Sifnos claimed that mallow tea has a palliative effect for the throat. Pythagora and his disciples had noticed that this plant refreshed the mind, boosted intuition and was easy to digest. The mallow leaves were combined with mashed bread crumbs to produce a paste that was used as cataplasm to treat skin diseases and frostbites. Similarly, medical practitioners in France and England would make a syrup to sooth the throat and comfort the respiratory system.

Mallow is rich in vitamins A, B1, C, B2 and can be added to chamomile tea to cure peptic disorders, constipation and inflammation of the respiratory system. Boiled and mashed

mallow leaves provide an excellent poultice for corns, gouty arthritis, acne, anaphylaxis, burns and insect bites.

◆ HARVEST – PURCHASE – STORAGE

Always pick tender mallow sprigs and leaves in early Spring, i.e. from late February to early April, because when the plant starts to blossom little larvae appear on the shoots. Flowers blossom in Spring, concurrently with chamomile. Mallows can be found almost anywhere: in gardens, fields, roadsides, etc. If you want them fresh you will have to pick them yourselves because you can rarely find them fresh in the market. In addition, mallow flowers are very seldom found in chamomile blends. To keep fresh mallow sprigs for 6-9 months, first clean them and heat water in a container. As soon as the water come to the boil add the mallow sprigs and let them boil for 2-3 minutes. Strain and let them cool before you place them in plastic bags and to the freezer. Mallow leaves are dried on a newspaper and in a cool and dark place.

◆ CULTURE

The mallow is a rather robust herbaceous and annual plant that is difficult to grow in pots, but can easily be found in fields. More than 16 species with flowers of various colours have been found in Europe.

◆ COOKING ◆

Those who love the taste of okras will also appreciate mallows. Mallow is scentless, and much like any other green. It combines well with sourish tastes. Peel mallow sprouts thoroughly as you would with fresh beans. Boil gently for approximately 4-5 minutes before serving them. Mallows can be cooked in casserole with chicken or lamb in tomato sauce and fit well with omelets, while the leaves are stuffed with rice and/or minced meat on the island of Crete.

In Cyprus the mallow leaves are used to make a soft-texture soup. Because of their small size and taste the mallow fruit is known as "buns" in Greece and "cookies" or "little cheese rolls" in southern Europe. They are eaten raw offering a pleasant, sweet taste.

MOUNTAIN TEA

— ❧ ❧ ❧ —

Sideritis spp.
Sideritis syriaca (Crete)
Sideritis euboea (Delphi)
Sideritis raeseri (Parnassos)
Sideritis cladestina (Peloponese)
Sideritis parxoliata (Mt. Athos)

The mountain tea is one of the most popular herbs in Greece. It has a pleasing taste and is said to aid digestion.

◆ MYTHOLOGY – HISTORY

This little bush grows on mountainous areas all over Greece and has been known since antiquity by the name "sideritis". Its name derives from the root noun "sideron", iron, and the plant is said to cure wounds effected by iron objects. You can find this herb in every nook and cranny on the island of Crete where it is also known as "malotiras", a complex noun from the Italian terms "male", illness, and "tirare", to pull. In other words the mountain tea pulls out or eradicates illness.

◆ POPULAR MEDICINE

The mountain tea is used to fight the common cold, infections of the respiratory system and persistent cough. It is considered ideal for stomach ache and indigestion. It was also used as a potent diuretic in case of kidney stones.

Laboratory analyses have shown that the small leaves and flowers of the mountain tea have significant amounts of flavonoid substances and essential oils.

◆ HARVEST – PURCHASE – STORAGE

In mid-summer, when the mountain tea is in full development, the top flowers and a few leaves are collected. To dry the mountain tea, collect the leaves and flowers and make a bunch of them. Then rig them up on a line in a cool and dry place. When the mountain tea is completely dry (6-8 days later), store it in airtight glass jars. The Greek markets offer ample quantities of mountain tea in various packages.

◆ CULTURE

A number of species of this plant are encountered on mountainous areas and track sides in all southern Europe, Greece, Spain, Portugal, Sicily, Malta, and Cyprus. This plant is cultivated in Cyprus where it is known by its ancient Greek name, "sideritis".

MARJORAM
A GARDEN HERB

— ❧ ❧ ❧ —

Origanum majorana
Origanum onites

◆ MYTHOLOGY – HISTORY

Evergreen marjoram probably originates from the Middle East. It was widely grown in Greece as early as antiquity, mainly for decorative purposes. However, the herb also found ample culinary and medicinal uses. The ancient Greeks used to make wreaths from this herb and crown the newly wedded couples, because they believed that the aroma from this plant was used by goddess Aphrodite. Ancient Egyptians, and later the Arabs, used marjoram extracts as tonic in their baths. Theophrastus claims that the peoples of Syria produced an intoxicating aroma from the leaves and flowers of marjoram.

◆ POPULAR MEDICINE

Singers and church cantors drunk marjoram tea with a little honey during the Middle Ages to sooth their throats and improve their vocal performance. In Greece marjoram was used as a medicinal herb against vertigo and vomiting. Chest ache owing to cold or stress was cured with marjoram tea where lemon rind was soaking. Marjoram is currently thought to fight indigestion, and stomach ache attributed to tension. Marjoram is excellent for soothing or relieving distress. Inhalation of marjoram vapors is very effective for people with bronchitis and blocked nostrils.

◆ HARVEST – PURCHASE– STORAGE

Marjoram is best if picked before it blossoms (May – June), otherwise the leaves will give a bitter taste. Dry it in a cool and dark place. You can make tea even from fresh marjoram leaves. If you buy it from your local market, choose marjoram stored in airtight jars or sealed in plastic bags. Store in a cool place.

◆ CULTURE

Marjoram is quite sensitive and can be grown from seeds or offshoots. It requires a lot of water and protection from the sun light and frost.

◆ COOKING ◆

For an authentic taste marjoram leaves are used fresh or dried with pork, chicken, omelets, casserole fish and meatball mixtures.

CHICORY
FOR A HEALTHY LIVER

— ❧ ❧ ❧ —

Cichorium intybus
Cichorium spinosum
Cichorium endivia

This is one of the most favourite greens in the broader region of the Mediterranean basin. It can be consumed in large quantities either raw, in salads, or cooked. It is an excellent tonic for the human body.

◆ MYTHOLOGY – HISTORY

Chicory is one of the "bitter herbs" and has been known since antiquity. The ancient Egyptians cultivated this vegetable systematically. The Greeks also acknowledged its nutritional value and consumed it regularly. Dioscurides (c. 512 AD) makes note of its diuretic qualities while Galinus calls it "friend of the liver", meaning that it cleanses the liver. In his text "Foods Beneficial to the People", Agapios Monachos the Cretan says that this plant with bright blue dandelion-like flowers is the best vegetable for people.

◆ POPULAR MEDICINE

Chicory is basically treated as a culinary herb. People on the island of Crete are accustomed to consuming large quantities of chicory,

either raw or boiled. The juice is said to invigorate the liver, has diuretic qualities and is recommended for people with diabetes.

In fact, it has been proved that boiled chicory provides a tonic which aids the flow of bile and is, therefore, recommended to people with stones in the gall-bladder.

The broth from boiled chicory, with a little olive oil and lemon juice, was considered an excellent concoction for blood "purification".

◆ HARVEST – PURCHASE – STORAGE

Chicory is found in the entire Mediterranean basin, and almost anywhere in Greece and the island of Crete. It grows by track sides, and uncultivated ground, valleys, even by the sea. The Chicorium spinosum species ("stamnagathi") abounds on Crete; it is delicious and very popular.

Depending on the type of soil they grow, chicory may be harvested all year round, however, during the summer its leaves are a little hard and exceptionally bitter. The best harvesting period is from early February to end April. In February you can collect the green leaves along with the white roots. In spring you collect the tender shoots before the plant blossoms. Chicory of all species is found in most markets of Greece, even in Supermarkets. To store chicory, place it in a plastic bag as soon as you bring it home from the market. Do not wash it. If you want to collect the leaves for

Cichorium spinosum
stamnagathi

drying and subsequent infusion making, follow the golden rule: first collect early in the morning, then dry in a cool and dark place.

◆ CULTURE

Chicory is easily cultivated from seeds. Sow early in winter on well-dug ground. Do not thin the plant (this is only for endives, Chicory endivia). You can also cultivate chicory by transplanting the little roots. Harvesting takes place the following year.

◆ COOKING ◆

The roots, tender leaves and shoots are served cooked or raw with a lot of olive oil and vinegar or lemon juice. The sweet chicory variety is cooked with meat. A delicious Cretan salad includes chicory as main ingredient accompanied with other sweet or aromatic herbs/greens. Chicory roots are dried, ground and used as substitute to coffee ("cafe cichore").

SAVORY
AN APHRODISIAC

— 🐌 🐌 🐌 —

Satureia hortensis
Satureia montana

A close relative to thyme, lavender, and sage (Lamiaceae plant family). This is a plant with delicate, mauve-pink flowers and small dark green leaves. It is very aromatic and found almost anywhere in Greece and Crete.

◆ MYTHOLOGY – HISTORY

The savory was used widely for digestion, following heavy meals, in the past. Cretan farmers would boil savory in large amounts of clear water that would later be used to wash and disinfect their wine barrels. The savory was also used for diarrhea, treatment of mouth sores, cold stomach and parasites of the intestines.

the blossomed flowers and dry them in a cool and dark place. Subsequently, you can pick a handful of dried flowers and rub them between your hands. Store the crumbled flowers in airtight jars. Fresh packed savory can be found in spice stores and large Supermarkets on Crete.

◆ CULTURE

This is possible from offshoots in rich soils. Allow 1-2 years for the plant to develop, then harvest.

◆ HARVEST – PURCHASE – STORAGE

In the countryside of Crete one can easily find the aromatic shrublet Satureia very easily. Pick

◆ COOKING ◆

The people of insular Greece would sprinkle savory over figs and raisins to keep them from deteriorating. The savory offers a peppery piquancy which marries well with game and grilled pork. It also adds flavour to vinegar which can later be used in marinades.

CHAMOMILE
THE INDISPENSABLE HERB

— 🌿 🌿 🌿 —

Marticaria chamolila

This is a little flower with white petals and scores of medicinal uses. You should always have a supply of chamomile sealed in airtight jars at home.

◆ MYTHOLOGY – HISTORY

Galinus extolled chamomile's antifebrile qualities and Dioscurides claimed that it also aids menstruation. Chamomile has been collected in Spring by women all over Greece and the Mediterranean for centuries.

◆ POPULAR MEDICINE

Popular medicine on Crete has it that bathing in chamomile water for about a month boosts fertility in women. Crushed chamomile in warm olive oil was used to sooth tummy aches and teething for babies. During the Middle Ages people would relax in baths of rosemary, chamomile and sage. A blend of four herbs boiled together constitute the "tea of happiness". These herbs are: the lemon plant, linden, mint, and chamomile.

Compresses of thick chamomile infusions are still customary on Crete for sore eyes. Fairly recent medical research has proved that chamomile is ideal for a wide range of pathological complaints. It heals wounds and burns; its acts as an anti-inflammatory and soothes eczema.

The chamomile tea relaxes and can induce sleep, particularly when combined with linden. It has a palliative effect on the muscles of the stomach, the intestine and the uterus. It is therefore recommended for peptic disorders. Chamomile compresses are also recommended for backache and treatment of the skin against dryness. Inhaling the vapors from a chamomile infusion it clears the bronchi and acts against acne of the face.

◆ HARVEST – PURCHASE – STORAGE

You can find chamomile almost anywhere in the country side in Spring – in fallow fields, dry, stony hillsides, etc. However, make sure that you collect it from places that you know are clean. Do not pick chamomile when the morning dew is still on its leaves, otherwise it will deteriorate soon. Keep it in pouches or jars that seal well. You can find ample quantities of chamomile in the local markets either in packages or jars.

◆ CULTURE

It grows easily from seeds that you sow in soft, limestone soils.

"ERONTAS-DITTANY"
THE MIRACULOUS HERB
OF CRETE

— ❧ ❧ ❧ —

Origanum dictammus

This hairy plant with round leaves and delicate flowers creeps along the steep slopes of Mt. Pseiloritis, Mt. Dikti and the White Mountains of Crete. Since Minoan times the "Erontas" was considered one of the most important medicinal herbs and was, therefore, exported to neighbouring islands.

◆ MYTHOLOGY – HISTORY

Another name for the ancient Cretan dictammus (dittany) was "Artemidion", referring to goddess Artemis who hunted with arrows dipped in poison. It is remarkable the fact that almost all ancient authors believed that dictammus had the quality to heal the wounds from poisoned arrow-heads. Dioscurides used the plant to heal combat wounds. He also mentions a particular wine where dictammus was used to add a particular fragrance. Aristotle mentions that wounded wild goats on Crete would expel arrows by chewing dictammus leaves. Virgil mentions that goddess Aphrodite healed Aeneas with only the application of Cretan dictammus on his wounds.

In his Obstetrics & Gynecology texts Aristotle claims that crushed dictammus leaves in warm water facilitates childbirth in pregnant women. Dictammus was exported to Byzantium for ointment and cataplasm preparations.

◆ POPULAR MEDICINE

Practical midwives on Crete used "Erontas" (or dictammus) cataplasms, teas and warm baths to facilitate deliveries. Mashed and mixed with water, it was also used as cataplasm for abscesses, boils, bruises and varices. It was also thought to facilitate menstruation. It is currently used as a stomach emollient, sedative, even as an aphrodisiac.

◆ HARVEST – PURCHASE – STORAGE

The fact that Dictammus grows on the steep mountain slopes on Crete makes collection not only difficult but also a dangerous operation. Small quantities of this plant have been identified by experts on the isles of Kassos and Cythera. Grown Dictammus is best in July when it is just starting to blossom and all fragrance gathers in the leaves. The Greek markets, particularly the Cretan, thrives in good quality, dried Dictammus. Purchase the plant in sealed packages or glass jars and store in a cool place. If you need to dry Dictammus, the golden rule of drying herbs applies here also: dry in a cool and dark place.

◆ CULTURE

You can easily grow Dictammus from seedlings that can be found in most nurseries on Crete. It requires a lot of sunlight, but moderate watering. The grown Dictammus is less aromatic in comparison with its wild counterpart.

◆ COOKING ◆

This herb has no culinary applications on the island of Crete. However, you can combine Dictammus with Marjoram and dried flowers of Mallow for a very tasty infusion.

CAPER

FOR APPETITE STIMULATION

— 🐚 🐚 🐚 —

Capparis spinosa

A small spiny shrub flourishing around the Mediterranean, mainly in walls and rocks near coastlines and barren plots.

♦ MYTHOLOGY – HISTORY

This shrub was often cited by the ancient Greeks and Romans who considered it more as condiment than vegetable. The Byzantines served it on a slice of bread with olive oil, vinegar and honey. The caper was also known as "evorekton" meaning appetizer plant and applied to sauces for fish and meat dishes.

♦ POPULAR MEDICINE

Dioscurides recommended cataplasms from caper leaves against swellings of the skin. In the Middle Ages caper infusions were considered aphrodisiac and a mild tonic.

Today we know that capparin, a constituent contained in the buds of this plant, stimulates the excretion of gastric fluids which are responsible for the sense of hunger.

♦ HARVEST – PURCHASE – STORAGE

Blossoms are to be harvested in the morning time, immediately before flowering, from May to July. The smaller buds, the size of small beans, are considered more valuable. However, you can harvest the fresh sprouts before May and the caper fruits, which are larger than the caper buds, after

August.

Today capers can be found growing wild all over the Mediterranean and are systematicaly cultivated in France, Spain, Italy, Algeria, Cyprus, Greece (insular complexes of the Cyclades and Dodekanese).

You can purchase fresh capers from your local market and make you own blend of pickles or preserve them in brine. Preserved capers can also be found in most supermarkets and are best kept in a refrigerator. Capers in vinegar are good for 2-3 years.

♦ CULTURE

There is no need to cultivate this plant since you can easily find it in your local market. Besides, to be able to collect enough caper fruits and buds you will have to grow a large number of plants.

♦ COOKING ♦

Owing to its pungent principle, capers are used to add flavour and colour to scores of meals popular in Italy and Spain. Capers are usually applied to salads with tomatoes and legumes (black-eyed beans). They are also cooked with pea puree or added to tomato sauces with a few raisins (Byzantine recipe).

In Italy capers are used a lot in spaghetti with anchovies, dried tomatoes and garlic, as well as in sauces for fish and meat dishes (rabbit and chicken). In Naples there is a popular dish of stuffed egg-plant with grated parmesan, bread, boiled eggs and plenty of capers. In Syria capers are consumed with coarse grain sea salt and barley bread. In France a boiled veal tongue meal is served with caper sauce. Capers go well with various bread preparations with oregano and marjoram.

FIGS

A SWEET FRUIT
WITH A LONG HISTORY

— ❧ ❧ ❧ —

In an extract from Text B of Athenaeus we read the following comment about the city-state of Athens: "Hipponicus, what wonderful things this land produces, distinguished all around the world: honey, bread, and figs. By god, it produces a lot of figs"

◆ MYTHOLOGY – HISTORY

However, the culinary master Archestratos considers dried figs base food and fit only for the poor folks: "You need not bother with those that consume the kinds of food that I advised you against. Such food, as for example boiled chickpeas, broad beans, apples and dried figs, are signs of destitution".

In antiquity dried figs and olives are cited in famous Pythagoreian dinners. Dried figs were referred to as royal *ischades* meaning figs kept in earthenware during the wintertime, as the peoples in the Mediterranean used to do until a few years ago. The Romans preserved figs in a different manner. Apicius said: "Choose those figs with their petioles, then place them in honey at some distance from each other".

◆ POPULAR MEDICINE

Hippocrates was well aware of the medicinal qualities of figs. Today we know that figs are beneficial to liver function, relieve coughs, asthma and pharyngitis. They are also used as diuretic. Those mindful of their silhouette should know that figs are high in sugar content. One hundred grams of figs contain approximately 80 cal, while dried figs contain more than 274 cal. each.

◆ HARVEST – PURCHASE – STORAGE

Depending on species, figs are harvested from April to November. Figs harvested in the beginning of spring are usually white in colour, i.e. have a light green skin and shiny red flesh. On the other hand, figs harvested during the summer have a dark violet skin, dark gold flesh and taste very sweet. In the heart of summer, the fruit markets around the Mediterranean offer excellent quality figs. Always buy figs ripe, this is because they do not ripe fast enough after harvest. Figs are best kept in the lower compartment of the refrigerator for up to 10-12 days. If the figs are too ripe and leave them outside the fridge, they will go sour fast.

♦ CULTURE

The prefecture of Attica is the home of the olive tree and fig tree. However, today fig trees are cultivated all around the Mediterranean. Large fig producing countries are: Algeria, Tunisia, Turkey, Libya, Spain, and S. Italy. Fig trees are usually grown by offshoots.

Figs from Smyrna and Aydin (Turkey) were quite famous. However, the best figs in the market today come from Inovassi (Turkey).

♦ COOKING ♦

Figs are not only preserved but also used to make a sweet drink, particularly in the Middle East during the period of Ramadan. In Kuwait, for example, this sweet drink is made by chopping the figs into little pieces which are then simmered with almonds, walnuts and ground cinnamon. The sweet drink, rather more like paste, is served cold.

In Turkey figs are usually served with fragrant vanilla and good quality brandy along with fresh yogurt. In Italy figs are stuffed with dried nuts and then kept in brandy. In Greece, dried figs, nuts, must and aromatic herbs are used as ingredients for excellent fig pies.

You can also make delicious marmalade from figs; however, this marmalade should be kept in refrigerators otherwise it will ferment very fast. Marmalade from figs is used to make tarts. White fig varieties (not very ripe) marry well with Parma ham and a glass of cool rose whine. The milky juice from fig trees is used for milk coagulation.

From 1955 to 1960 fat, lower quality figs were exported from Smyrna to Germany where they were processed to produce the famous Feigen Kaffe.

POMEGRANATE
THE MEDITERRANEAN
FRUIT OF THE GODS

— ❧ ❧ ❧ —

Punica granatum

Its seed are a symbol of fertility, prosperity, and hope.

Pomegranate's almost transparent and shiny seeds are in

full maturity in autumn, the onset of the calendar year

for the ancients.

♦ MYTHOLOGY – HISTORY

In antiquity the pomegranate was attributed magical qualities (e.g fertility) and associated with goddesses Demeter, Aphrodite and Hera. For Demeter, the seeds stored only sorrow and bad luck: that was when her daughter Persephone ate from the pomegranates of the dead. In spite of this association, Athenian women ate pomegranate seeds in ceremonies ("Thesmoforia") during the celebrations in honour of goddess Demeter to entreat fertility and prosperity.

Aphrodite, on the other hand, is said to be the one who planted the pomegranate tree on the island of Cyprus. However, according to myths, Hera, the patroness of marriage and birth, and pomegranates form a closer fit. In the town of Argos there are the remains of an ancient temple of Hera where, according to

myth, Pausanias marveled at the ivory-gold statue of the goddess holding a pomegranate in her right hand.

In Iran people believe that the pomegranate tree is a gift of the gods. In the Koran prophet Mohammed is quoted as follows: "Eat pomegranates because they purge the mind of envy and hatred".

In Greek the pomegranate fruit is "Rodi", while different versions are also used in various parts of the country, e.g. "Roa" or "Roia". These probably originate from the Arabic equivalent "Roumman". In Boeotia and Crete the names "Sidi" or "Sida" were also used during the last century. This fruit is also cited by Homer, Theophrastus, Dioscurides and Pliny.

◆ POPULAR MEDICINE

Hippocrates recommended the juice of pomegranates as aphrodisiac and stomach sedative. Dioscurides and Pliny recommended infusions from the root and skin of pomegranates against the parasites of the intestines. In modern times the pomegranate fruit is used in cases of diarrhea, dysentery, and vaginal infection. A mixture of pomegranate juice and olive oil is used to treat skin spots. The antioxidant qualities of the juice are exploited by modern cosmetology in the designed of products to eliminate facial wrinkles. A thick herbal pomegranate tea is used for gargles to treat sore throats.

◆ HARVEST – PURCHASE – STORAGE

The pomegranates are best when mature with the first rains in early February. Harvesting them from trees is easy. Pomegranates have a long shelf life and even longer when refrigerated. The seeds are more juicy and good to eat even when the skin appears wrinkled. A popular method of storage is hanging them in bunches from their stems in a dark place around the house. Pomegranates vary in taste from sweet to sour.

◆ CULTURE

The pomegranate tree grows in sunny warm terrains and thrives in the Mediterranean basin. It propagates by offshoot-grafts and develops easily. The first yield comes three years later. It blossoms from May to July.

◆ COOKING ◆

The sweet-sour molasses from pomegranate's seeds adds a unique flavour to meals. These molasses are known as "nastrab" in Georgia (Russian Republic) where they make a very tasty dish with fish, egg-plants and pomegranate juice, the "Ruman" in the Middle East and "Nar" in Turkey.

The pomegranate's juice is used in various ways around the world. It is mixed with walnuts, added to poultry dishes, and marries well with tender lamb and pork meat. It is included in a Lebanese casserole okra dish and in a Persian dish with chicken legs, walnuts, saffron, fresh butter and aromatic rose petals.
Fresh pomegranate seeds are used in salads with wild greens (chicory, endives) in Crete. Canned juice is sold in Lebanon, Turkey and Persia.

QUINCE
THE FRAGRANT AUTUMN FRUIT

— 🍃 🍃 🍃 —

Cydonia vulgaris | Each October we notice this fragrant fruit in the local markets of Greece. It is of a fine handsome shape of rich golden colour when ripe, with a strong, overpowering fragrance. It is used both for meal and pastry preparations.

◆ MYTHOLOGY – HISTORY

The remains of a 4000 year old quince cultivation were found in Persia (now Iran). Centuries later the quince became the symbol of Love and Happiness, a gift of goddess Gaea to goddess Hera on the day the latter wedded to Zeus.

During classical antiquity the Greeks cultivated at least ten varieties of this fruit. The most famous of those varieties were cultivated in Crete and Corinth. The Romans kept quinces in a mixture of thick honey and molasses juice. During the Middle Ages the quince was the favourite ingredient for the French, Portuguese and Spanish confectionery.

◆ POPULAR MEDICINE

Dioscurides mentions that quinces raise the appetite and comfort the stomach. During the Palladius (4thc. AD) recommends the juice of quinces mixed with honey, vinegar and spices to those suffering from mild anorexia. The monks at Mt. Athos take the juice of quinces to fight cough and heart burns.

The seeds of quinces were used by practical physicians to make cough syrup while seeds boiled in olive oil were used to fight loss of hair (alopecia).

◆ HARVEST – PURCHASE – STORAGE

Ripe quinces are available in the Greek fruit markets from September to December. Their shelf life is approximately 10 days, but they can be maintained in the fridge for more than 20 days.

◆ CULTURE

The quince tree is cultivated quite easily from scion grafts in rich and moist soils. The tree yields fruit three years later and blossoms from April to June.

◆ COOKING ◆

For years now Greek women have been fascinated with the discrete look of this fruit and experimented with it in their kitchen. They use it to make a delicious preserve and jelly, ruby-like in colour. One of the many recipes with quince in the Middle East is one which involves baking quinces at low temperature with honey, sweet wine, cinnamon and carnation cloves.

Quinces are also delicious in casserole while their sour rind harmonizes perfectly with pork, tender lamb, veal and duck.

LEEK

ALLIED SPECIES TO ONION AND GARLIC

— 🥬 🥬 🥬 —

Allium porrum

In a 15th century manuscript we read the following exhortation discouraging people from consuming leeks, "…it is the least fortunate of all vegetables that should not be consumed by slender people, but only by those who are strong in constitution and the labourers…" Such exhortations were not enough to halt the cultivation and wide application of leeks

♦ MYTHOLOGY – HISTORY

How old is the gastronomic history of this "heavy smelling" vegetable, the leek? The Romans believed that the best of leeks could be found in Egypt. Ancient Greek texts thrive in references to this tasty vegetable ("kromion to prasso") which was cultivated owing to its pungent taste. An ancient sauce, the "myttotos", was made from soft cheese, grated garlic, olive oil, leeks and honey. For centuries the leek was very popular with Greek chanters who believed that their sweet constituents improved the tone of their voice.

♦ POPULAR MEDICINE

Leeks are rich in minerals, iron, vitamins and make excellent tonic, antiseptic and antiemetic infusions. Owing to their rich sensoric qualities, leeks promote intestine function and increase appetite. In ancient Greece, leeks were also applied to cases of food poisoning.

♦ HARVEST – PURCHASE – STORAGE

Harvesting wild or cultivated leeks is rather easy. Leeks are easily distinguishable among other vegetables owing to their long size. Fresh produce markets offer leeks in early autumn. Wild leeks are usually found growing in uncultivated plots and vineyards from December to April. When purchasing leeks make sure that the white, root-side part, is firm and the green part is fresh. To keep leeks fresh, place them in a plastic bag and store them in the lower compartment of your refrigerator. Alternatively, you can peel, chop and place the pieces in plastic bags and store them in the fridge for 2-3 days. Do not wash them first. Or, you can buy the quantities you require for 6-7 months, peel, chop and slightly boil them in salted water before you store them in the freezer.

♦ CULTURE

Leeks are easily cultivated from seeds. Sowing takes place in August, but leeks also grow from seedlings in rich soils.

♦ COOKING ♦

The popularity of leek is the result of its versatile culinary application. It mixes harmoniously with fish, meat, legumes and vegetables.
In northern Greece leeks are used in pies made from cheese, eggs and other herbs. Popular dishes with leeks are: salted cod, veal, pork with quince. Leeks are also added in salads, soups and tarts. Wild leeks have a milder taste than cultivated leeks.

ROSE

A CULINARY FLOWER

—— ❧ ❧ ❧ ——

Rosa canina
Rosa gallica officinalis
Rosa rubigi - nosa
Rosa damascena

Sung by ancient Greek scholars, Homer, Sappho and Anacreon, the rose truly deserves the title of king of ornamental cultivars and confectionery ingredients.

♦ MYTHOLOGY – HISTORY

In ancient Greece the rose was the flower of Arpocratus, the god of silence, and a symbol of secrecy. The hosts of symposia would rig a garland of roses in the hall where an after-dinner discussion was to take place and participants were to be in complete confidence of the matters discussed. One more myth says that the rose was born from nectar that was accidentally spilled by little god Pothos ("Desire") dancing among the Olympian gods during a feast. In one of his myths Ovid says that the rose was born from the blood of Adonis. The myths above indicate that roses were known and used in antiquity. Information about oils extracted from roses were found inscribed on clay tablets in the palace of Cnossos.

The Romans were the first to cultivate roses in closed gardens and exploited the fragrant rose petals for culinary and confectionery applications. The ancient Greeks used roses for cosmetic purposes. Roman Apicius cites a recipe entitled "A panful of rose petals". The Roman culinary applications of roses were bequeathed to the Byzantines who sprinkled rosewater and blossom water over meat and pastries.

♦ POPULAR MEDICINE

Rose fruits are rich in vitamin C and used for tea preparations in the Middle East and China. In the past owing to its antibacterial qualities, the pulp from rose petals was used in the cure of wounds. The essential oil in the petals is considered an aphrodisiac and used for massages and in aromatherapy. The rose-essence contains more than 300 different chemical substances. For popular Indian medicine, the rose essence and rose tea are strong tonics for the mind.

◆ HARVEST – PURCHASE – STORAGE

May is the best month of the year, at least in Greece, to harvest roses to make preserves, rosewater, and marmalades, or mix petals with vinegar. Choose the semi-wild variety of roses with pink coloured petals. Harvest them during morning hours when they are fresh and most fragrant.

Before using them, remove the nectary (whitish narrower tip of petal). If the quantity of petals you collected the first time is not enough, then place the first harvest in a plastic bag and store it in the lower compartment of the refrigerator. Supplement this quantity in the next couple of days. Refrigerated rose petals retain their fragrance for at least three days.

◆ CULTURE

References to roses in ancient Greece and Rome are references to the wild variety, the fragrant *Rosa carina*. Currently more than 2000 rose varieties have been recorded around the world. Roses are easy to cultivate from grafts in soft and rich soils.

◆ COOKING ◆

By far the most important source of essential oil is the Central Asian species *Rosa damascena* (Damaskus rose). This gives also excellent rosewater that is used for the production of sweet drinks (sherbet), ice-creams, etc. The deep red petals of this species are even consumed raw or slightly boiled in rice.

The green leaves and flowers of this variety are used as condiment, "Bacharat", in meat dishes. In Greece, the fragrant petals of the May rose species are used to make the "rodosachari" are preserve offered as a treat to visitors of monasteries in Peloponense, Dodekanese, the Cyclades and Crete. Rose petals were also used to add fragrance to vinegar and produce the "rodoxino" which is used even today for dressing salads and potatoes.

GRAPES
A GIFT OF DIONYSUS
TO THE PEOPLE

— ?♣ ?♣ ?♣ —

For the people of the Mediterranean basin, grapes

are the most significant fruit and

the resulting wine a universal drink throughout

the world from very early times.

♦ MYTHOLOGY – HISTORY

The history concerning the appearance of the vine in the Mediterranean is lost in time and myth. In the Scriptures the vine is frequently mentioned from the time of Noah onwards. According to Greek mythology it was god Dionysus who gave vine arbours as present to the son of a satyr by the name "Ampelos". A different version of the myth says that Dionysus presented the first vine root to "Oeneas", king of Caledonia.

Vine cultivation was a very significant agricultural activity both for ancient Greeks and Romans. Pliny speaks of the wine as "a supreme good by the gods to the people that should be taken in moderation, if it is to nourish the body and soul". Homer also speaks of the wines that accompanied the meals of gods and mortals. He recommended moderation and the mixing of wines with two parts of water. According to Athenaeus the best wines were produced on the isles of Samos, Thassos, Chios, and Crete. The ancient Greeks were very keep on improvising with wine varieties. They were also familiar with the culinary and confectionery application of other vine products (must, leaves, raisins). For example, Athenaeus provided us with a list of aromatic herbs, such as the coriander, leek, thyme, sage. Among them he included molasses from grape juice. Apicius also mentions a recipe of African must-cakes which are scraped with a knife and then dipped in milk and honey.

◆ POPULAR MEDICINE

Owing to their nutritional and medicinal qualities grapes are very popular around the world. During the Roman period physicians prescribed the "grape cure" to sufferers from torpid liver. Wine mixed with aromatic herbs, such as the sage, thyme, etc., was extensively used to disinfect wounds and as tonic.

The constituents of grapes (75-83% water, 1.7% nitrogenous combinations, 1.3% mineral salts, and 12-30% sugar) is comparable to those of maternal milk (87% water, 0.1-1.5% nitrogenous combinations, 0.4% mineral salts, 11% sugar). Molasses from grapes was used extensively in the past to cure whooping cough and fatigue. Molasses combined with olive oil is an excellent nutrient.

◆ HARVEST – PURCHASE – STORAGE

The ripe time for harvesting grapes depends on the location of vineyards and mode of cultivation. In any case grapes are harvested from May to November. In local markets you can find different varieties of grapes almost all year round. Raisins are packaged airtight and sold in special stores. The molasses are packaged in small glass jars and maintained outside the refrigerator for 2-3 years. Grapes are best maintained (1-2 weeks) in plastic bags and stored in the lower compartment of the refrigerators.

Fresh grapes can also be preserved in brandy or vodka. The must is kept in freezers for about a year.

◆ COOKING ◆

The savoro fish recipe, which is popular in mainland Greece and the isles of Zakynthos and Tenos, is accompanied with a sauce made from molasses, vinegar and raisins. The Turkish uzleme dish, lamb with rice and chickpeas, is served with molasses sauce.

The Asian Minor cuisine uses molasses as dressing in pastries, e.g. in puddings. Raw grapes are popular all over the world. Raw grapes with feta or other cheese and a couple of slices of bread make an excellent breakfast.

A fairly unknown traditional Cretan recipe is rice cooked with fresh tomatoes and served with a lot of grape fruits. This is usually served during periods of fasting.

The Spanish *Ozo Blanco* soup also includes peeled raw grapes. Raw grapes are also added to green salads.

Raisins also have culinary and confectionery applications. They are added to bread, cakes and used as stuffing for turkey, pheasant and duck dishes.

LEEK

WARM SALAD WITH LEEK AND THYME

Serves 6
7 large, tender leeks
2 cloves garlic
4 tomatoes, finely sliced (not peeled)
3 tbsp olive oil
1 tsp thyme
4 tbsp dry white wine
Salt
Pepper

1. Clean, wash and slice the leeks into 5 cm pieces. Boil the leek slices in a pot with salted water for 15 min. until tender.
2. Warm olive oil in a heavy bottom frying pan and fry garlic gently until softened, not browned.
3. Remove and dispose of garlic, add the tomatoes, thyme and wine. Stir gently and simmer for approximately 10 min. Then add the salt and pepper, stir gently and taste the sauce. It should be a little thick. Remove leeks from pot with perforated spoon and let them strain in a colander; place them in large dish and pour the hot sauce over.

LEEK-PIE

Serves 8
Pastry sheets (filo), 1 kg
3 tbsp olive oil

Stuffing:
Leeks (remove green sections) finely chopped, 2 kg
Dill, 1 bunch finely chopped
Feta cheese (hard), grated, 500 gr
1 cup Pecorino cheese, grated
1 cup yogurt, strained
5 eggs
30 gr butter
1 tbsp semolina
Salt
Pepper

1. Clean leeks and remove the green section, then cut in four crosswise from top to bottom and chop finely with sharp knife. Place the pieces in a colander and rinse them well. Allow leek pieces to strain completely. Melt the butter in a deep frying pan and stir-fry the leeks for 10 minutes until tender, not browned. Remove pan from oven ring to let the leeks cool off.
2. Strain leeks from excess butter, then place them in a large bowl and add the cheese, dill, semolina, eggs

(whisked), salt, pepper. Stir all using two forks.

3. Choose a rectangular (50x28 cm) or round (60-70 cm in diam.) baking pan and slightly grease with melted butter. Spread 4 filo pastry sheets and brush their surfaces with butter. Place half the stuffing and top it with one or two pastry sheets.

4. Add the rest of the stuffing and on top of it 5 more pastry sheets. Roll the sheet edges inward and curve the pie in rhomboid fashion. Sprinkle the pie surface with ample butter and bake in oven at 170ºC for 50 minutes.

CREAMY LEEK SOUP

Serves 6
3 large leeks, finely chopped
75 gr butter
2 tbsp flour
6 cups chicken stock
2 eggs (only the yolks)
3 tbsp fresh cream
salt
pepper, freshly ground

1. Gently sauté the leeks in butter until tender and slightly "transparent" (do not allow them to turn brown)

2. Add the flour and stir vigorously with wooden ladle for 3-4 minutes. Add the stock immediately and bring to the boil, then lower temperature to simmer for 20 more minutes. Sprinkle salt and pepper to your satisfaction.

3. Strain and collect the soup in a colander. Put half the leeks in a food processor and process until they turn pulpy. Pour the stock in a clean casserole, add the remaining sliced leeks and pulp. Stir well and bring the mixture to the boil.

4. Turn off oven ring and whisk the yolks gently, add the crème in the casserole and continue whisking the yolks for 4-5 minutes. Pour the mixture in soup stirring well and serve immediately.

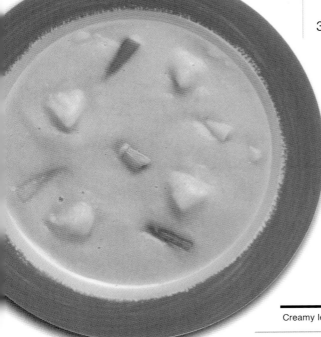

Creamy leek soup

BASIL

SARDINES WITH BASIL AND OLIVE PASTE

Serves 6
1 kg large sardines
2 cups of olive oil
1 cup flour
1 cup breadcrumbs
1 egg
Salt
Pepper

Stuffing:
6 finely chopped black olives or 1 tbsp olive paste.
1 tbsp finely chopped fresh basil
1 tsp finely chopped sweet red pepper

1. Choose large sardines and remove their heads. Wash them thoroughly, salt and let them dry completely.
2. Slice the sardines open to remove the bones – do not halve.
3. Mix olive paste (or chopped olives) with the finely chopped pepper and fill the sardines with the mixture. Fold sardines back and flour each one by one, then dip each first in the flour, then in the whisked egg, and finally in the breadcrumbs.
4. Bring the olive oil to the boil and brown the sardines on both sides. Serve with ample lemon juice.

PEPPERS IN BAKING TIN WITH CHEESE AND BASIL

Serves 10
1 ½ kg red peppers
1 ½ soft feta cheese
4 tbsp sweet soft cheese ("mizithra") or Philadelphia cheese
2 tbsp basil, finely chopped
4 tbsp olive oil, extra virgin
1 tsp vinegar
1/2 green pepper
Salt

1. Rinse peppers under running water and place them on the oven rack to cook at 180ºC until tender.
2. In a small bowl mix the finely chopped basil with two tablespoons of olive oil, the vinegar, and a little salt. Beat the mixture with a fork to mix well.
3. Pick a second bowl and add the cheese, the remaining two tablespoons of olive oil, the

pepper, and mix very well.

4. Take peppers out of the oven and cover them with a thin film. Allow them to cool down. Remove their skins carefully, deseed and shred them with your fingers in two pieces. Drizzle the pepper filets with a little olive oil.

5. Pick an oblong baking tin and line it with a thin film that extends about an inch beyond the tin edges. Cover the tin bottom with a layer of a few pepper filets. Top filets with a little basil mixture and then a thin layer of the cheese mixture which you apply with a slightly oiled spatula.

6. Continue with another layer of peppers, herbs and cheese. Finish with a layer of peppers. The thickness of the preparation should be approximately 6-7 cm. Place the baking tin in the refrigerator for 7-8 hours.

7. Remove the tin from the refrigerator when you are ready to serve. Topple the baking tin as is over a large dish, with transparent film extending from the edges. Remove baking tin and film carefully so that the meal maintains its form.

8. Choose a sharp knife to cut thin slices. Serve with green salad.

CHIOS EGG-PLANTS WITH FETA CHEESE AND BASIL

Servers 4
4 egg-plants, medium size
6 tbsp feta cheese, hard type sliced in cubes
4 cloves garlic, crushed
2 tbsp olive oil
1 tbsp fresh basil

1. Place egg-plants over charcoal or on the oven grill and cook both sides well. Pick a pointed knife and curve along egg-plants to let the juice strain out. Mix the feta cheese cubes, parsley, garlic and olive oil in a bowl.

2. Fill the egg-plants with the stuffing from the bowl. Close egg-plants and place them on grill again for 10 minutes, or until the feta cheese melts. Serve egg-plants open as soon as you take them out of the oven.

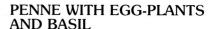
PENNE WITH EGG-PLANTS AND BASIL

Serves 8
1 packet of penne or other hollow pasta
3 egg-plants
200 gr. feta cheese
4 tbsp parmesan cheese, grated
2 eggs
a few basil leaves
pepper, freshly ground
800 gr fresh tomatoes, peeled
1 onion, grated
½ tsp garlic
1 tbsp sugar
1/4 cup olive oil

1. Peel and cut the egg-plants in small cubes. Let them rest in a bowl with salted water for 2-3 hours, then strain and fry them well in olive oil. When ready, remove from pan and place them on absorbent kitchen paper in a large dish.
2. Prepare the sauce with the tomatoes, onion, garlic, sugar and olive oil. When the sauce is thick, let it cool down. Grate the feta cheese.
3. Boil the penne for two minutes and let them cool off. Transfer the penne to a large pyrex container and stir in the sauce, egg-plants, feta cheese, pepper and basil. Cover with foil, check if the contents are juicy enough, and bake in preheated over at 180ºC. Break the eggs in a bowl and whisk in 4 tablespoons of water and the parmesan.
4. As soon as the penne come to the boil, remove the foil, pour the mixture of eggs all over and bake in the oven until a nice crust forms. Serve immediately.

Chios egg-plants with feta cheese and basil.

TUNA IN TOMATO AND BASIL SAUCE

Serves 4
2 tbsp olive oil
1 large onion sliced thinly
$1/4$ cup of finely chopped celery
$1/4$ cup of very finely chopped basil
1 clove of finely chopped garlic
1 large ripe tomato, peeled and roughly sliced
1 laurel leaf
1 cup fresh basil, roughly cut
4-6 tuna fish chunks
sprigs of basil

1. Warm one tablespoon of olive oil in a large, heavy bottom pan at moderate heat. Add the onions, celery, chopped basil and garlic. Stir-fry for 10 minutes until the onion is soft, not brown. Add the tomatoes and the laurel leaf. Cover the pan and cook for approximately 15 minutes, until the sauce is thick. Stir occasionally.
2. Remove and dispose of the laurel leaf. Add the chopped basil, salt and pepper to the mixture.
3. Sprinkle the tuna chunks with salt and pepper. Again, warm the remaining 1 tbsp of olive oil in another large, heavy pan over moderate heat. Then empty the tuna chunks in the pan and cook until golden, approximately 3 minutes for each side.
4. Transfer the tuna to a large dish. Pour the sauce over the tuna and garnish with fresh basil sprigs.

Tuna in tomato and basil sauce

BOILED POTATOES IN BASIL SAUCE

Servers 6
1 kg of small potatoes
salt

Sauce:
2 tbsp fresh basil leaves, finely chopped
1 tsp fresh mint leaves, finely chopped
2 anchovies, washed thoroughly
1 tbsp capers
4 tbsp extra virgin olive oil
1 tbsp fresh lemon juice
½ tsp pepper

1. Boil the potatoes in a lot of salted water. When done, strain the potatoes and keep them warm aside.
2. Put the olive oil, anchovies, basil, mint, pepper and lemon juice in the blender.
3. Process at medium speed for 1-2 minutes until you get a fine thick sauce. Add the capers and mix well.
4. Serve the potatoes in warm plates and pour the sauce over.

TOMATO SOUFLE WITH BASIL

Serves 4
½ ripe tomatoes sliced thinly
3 tbsp finely chopped fresh basil
4 eggs, whisked
250 gr milk
1 tbsp sugar
1 tsp salt
butter
nutmeg

1. Fry the tomatoes at low temperature for 15 minutes, or until soft. Squash tomatoes with fork, then add the basil.
2. Preheat oven at 180°C. Whisk the eggs with the sugar, milk and salt and spoon in the tomato purée.
3. Butter 4 small earthenware soufflé forms and pour in the mixture. Sprinkle with nutmeg, place in ben-mari and cook in the oven at 180°C for 20 minutes.

OIL & VINEGAR SAUCE WITH BASIL FOR FRIED EGG-PLANTS

½ cup of extra virgin olive oil
4 tbsp vinegar
2 tbsp lemon juice
4 cloves garlic
1 tsp fresh basil, chopped finely
1 tsp salt
2-3 drops of lukewarm water

1. Crush the garlic with the salt in mortar. Pour this pulp in a large bowl or airtight glass jar along with the rest of the ingredients.
2. Beat/Shake well until all ingredients mix well.

BASIL IN OLIVE OIL
(You can use the oil to pour over roast and pasta dishes)

Basil (as much as you like)
Olive oil

1. Wash basil sprigs and dry them completely. Cut sprigs to smaller pieces and place them in small jars pressing them slightly to fill jar.
2. Pour in the olive oil to fill the jar and seal tightly. Store in a cool place.

BASIL IN OLIVE OIL

(You can use the oil to pour over roast and pasta dishes)
Basil (as much as you like) Olive oil

1. Wash basil sprigs and dry them completely. Cut sprigs to smaller pieces and place them in small jars pressing them slightly to fill jar.
2. Pour in the olive oil to fill the jar and seal tightly. Store in a cool place.

OREGANO

TOMATO BALLS
(a la Santorini)

Serves 6
3 large and ripe
tomatoes
1 large onion,
finely chopped
1 tsp oregano
1 tsp baking
powder
1 cup flour (or 2-3
tbsp more)
salt

1. Halve and deseed the tomatoes, place them in blender and turn on/off the switch (3-4 times) until the tomatoes are sliced to little pieces, but not turned into pulp.
2. Empty the sliced tomato in a fine colander and let them drain completely, approx. 1 hour.
3. Mix the tomatoes in a bowl with the onion, oregano, baking powder, salt, pepper and flour. The mixture should be thick, if not, add as much flour as its takes.
4. Pour the olive oil in large non stick frying pan and warm well. With a tablespoon take the tomato mixture scoop-by-scoop and empty it in hot olive oil.
5. Fry the tomato balls at high temperature until brown on both sides
6. When the tomato balls are ready, pick a large dish, cover it with kitchen paper and place the tomato balls. Serve immediately.

LAMB IN OLIVE OIL & OREGANO

Serves 6
1 ½ kg lamb
1 cup olive oil
1 tsp oregano
1 tsp salt
3/4 cup wine
pepper

1. Wash lamb and slice it in small pieces. Warm olive oil in large saucepan and sauté the meat on all sides until well brown.
2. Pour the wine over the meat, sprinkle with the oregano, salt, pepper, and add 2 cups of water. Cover saucepan with lid and simmer for 50 minutes at low temperature. Check water from time to time.
3. Serve hot with French fries and salad.

WINTER SOUP WITH MIXED MEAT AND WILD OREGANO

Serves 10
½ kg veal (neck)
½ kg lamb (neck)
½ chicken
1 tsp wild oregano (fresh or dried)
1 clove garlic, crushed
1 tbsp finely chopped parsley
5 tbsp flour
2 eggs
1 tsp fresh butter
1 tbsp lemon juice
salt
pepper

1. Boil meat in a large casserole with 2 lt of water for 1 ½ hours. Remove the casserole lid during the last half hour.

2. Put the meat into a colander and collect the stock in a pan. Remove and dispose bones and place boneless meat in the stock. Add salt, parsley, garlic (crushed) and simmer the stock for 10 minutes. Take two cups of stock and pour in a bowl. Allow the stock there to cool off before mixing it with the flour. Pour this mixture back into the pan, stir vigorously and simmer for 6-7 minutes. Add the oregano, the warm butter, cover pan with lid and let the soup rest for 5 minutes. Stir in well the whisked eggs in the pan. Serve immediately.

A simple but tasty soup flavoured with spicy oregano buds just before the flower.

FISH ON THE SPIT WITH OREGANO

Serves 6
1 ½ kg squids or cuttlefish*,
cleaned
100 gr. white breadcrumbs
the peel from 2 green
lemons (squeeze lemons
first)
3 cloves fresh garlic
1 glass dry white wine
1 bunch parsley
1 bunch oregano
extra virgin olive oil
salt
pepper

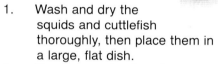

1. Wash and dry the squids and cuttlefish thoroughly, then place them in a large, flat dish.
2. For your marinade, mix the oregano, lemon peel (grated), wine, a few drops of olive oil, salt, and pepper. Marinade the squids and cuttlefish in cool environment for a few hours. Stir occasionally.
3. In a non-stick frying pan add a little olive oil and spoon in the breadcrumbs to fry for 1 minute until golden. Peel and crush the garlic, finely chop the parsley and mix them with the breadcrumbs for 1 minute.
4. Remove squids and cuttlefish from marinade and pat them dry with kitchen paper. Roll them in the mixture of bread crumbs, pierce them with sticks and grill them on both sides in preheated oven for 5-6 minutes. Occasionally brush

the "souvlakia" with olive oil.
Serve hot as soon as ready.
* For better cooking results, it is important that the seafood be of small size.

STUFFED TOMATOES WITH BARLEY HARD BREAD AND OLIVE OIL

Serves 6
10 tbsp extra virgin olive oil
4 small tomatoes, preferably pomontori
½ tsp tomato paste
2 cups ground barley hard bread
1 cup parsley, finely chopped
2 cloves garlic, finely chopped
2 eggs, whisked
1 tsp oregano
2 tbsp hard cheese ("kefalotyri")
salt
1 tsp black pepper

1. Wash, let dry and halve the tomatoes. Pick a teaspoon, remove but retain a little of their flesh. Sprinkle tomatoes with salt and turn them over to let juice/water drain for 20 minutes.
2. Mix the breadcrumbs, tomato paste, tomato flesh, parsley, garlic, oregano, cheese, eggs and pepper. Stuff tomatoes with this mixture and place them in pyrex dish with slightly oiled bottom. Pour a tablespoon of olive oil over each tomato and cook at 200°C for 20 minutes.

ROSEMARY

BREAD RINGS WITH ONIONS AND ROSEMARY

1 ½ cup olive oil
2 cups flour
15 gr. fresh yeast
2 tbsp butter
2 large red onions, finely chopped
3 spring onions, finely chopped
1 tbsp fresh rosemary
1 tsp salt
1 tbsp coarse grain sea salt
1 tbsp sugar

1.   Pick a large bowl and pour flour in. Make a cavity in the middle of the flour where you add the salt, yeast (dissolved in warm water), olive oil and a little sugar. Kneed the mixture gradually adding a little warm water until the mixture turns a little elastic. Transfer the mixture to a slightly floured surface and kneed again. Transfer the mixture to a clean bowl, cover with napkin and let stand for 20-25 minutes.
2.   Divide the dough into pieces, kneed each piece to form medium size rolls. Place rolls on large baking pan that has been brushed with olive oil. Press on rolls with your palm to flatten their surface.
3.   Warm one half cup of olive oil in a frying pan and sauté the finely chopped red onions until slightly brown. Remove onions using a perforated spoon and place them in small colander to strain their olive oil.
4.   Take a tablespoon of finely chopped red onions and spread it on the rolls, pressing

them slightly to stick in. Sprinkle with a little sugar, coarse grain sea salt and rosemary. Preheat oven at 180°C and bake for 50-60 minutes. Serve the bread rings warm or cold.

LEG OF LAMB IN SALT WITH ROSEMARY

Serves 6
1 leg of lamb, approx. 2 kg.
1 tbsp rosemary
1 cup white wine, unresinated
2 ½ kg coarse grain salt
pepper

1.   Wash leg of lamb thoroughly, without removing the bone nor

The tender meat of lamb enriched with fragrant rosemary. All the meat juices and the herb flavour are trapped inside due to the thick layer of coarse grain seasalt.

the white membrane lining the surface. Let the leg stand to dry.

2. Wash the lamb leg a second time in wine. Pour the rest of wine on lamb and sprinkle with the rosemary.

3. Spread a layer of coarse grain salt, approx. 2 cm thick, in a large baking pan. Place the lamb leg on top of that layer and cover with a thick layer of coarse grain salt.

4. Place baking pan with lamb in the middle of the oven and bake at 200°C for approximately two hours. Subsequently, remove baking dish from the oven, break the crust of salt and serve the lamb with a lot of green salad.

SNAILS IN ROSEMARY

Serves 4
20 snails in their shells
½ cup olive oil
2 tsp salt
3 tbsp strong,
red vinegar
1 tsp
rosemary

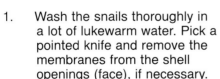

1. Wash the snails thoroughly in a lot of lukewarm water. Pick a pointed knife and remove the membranes from the shell openings (face), if necessary.

2. Place a non-stick frying pan on oven ring and sprinkle its bottom with 1 tablespoon of salt. Place each snail face down in the pan and fry without stirring at high temperature for 4-5 minutes. Sprinkle the rest of the salt over snails and add the olive

oil. Continue frying at moderate temperature for another 5-6 minutes.

3. Pick a fork and stir snails in the pan, sprinkle with rosemary and pour the vinegar all over the snails. Let the snails "boil" in vinegar for 1-2 minutes and then remove the frying pan from the oven ring. Serve snails hot in their juice.

BABY POTATOES IN ROSEMARY

Serves 8
20-30 round, baby potatoes
1 cup olive oil
1 tbsp rosemary
salt

1. Peel and wash potatoes well. Warm the olive oil in a frying pan and add the potatoes. Stir immediately and cover the pan with lid.

2. Fry for 3-4 minutes until potatoes are slightly brown. Remove the pan from oven ring and sprinkle the potatoes with rosemary. Remove potatoes from the pan with perforated spoon and place them on a large dish, over kitchen paper to absorb their oil. Sprinkle salt over the potatoes and serve immediately.

LOBSTER IN VIRGIN OLIVE OIL, GARLIC AND ROSEMARY

Serves 4
1 fresh/frozen lobster, medium size
olive oil, ½ wine glass
lemon juice from 1 lemon
1 tsp rosemary
1 clove garlic, crushed
1 glass of water
salt
pepper

1. Boil the lobster in a large pan with ample salted water at high temperature for 25-40 minutes.
2. When done, take lobster out of the pan, remove the shell and cut lobster into chunks. Pick a frying pan to accommodate the lobster chunks, add the water, garlic, olive oil, lemon juice and sprinkle with the salt and pepper. Allow the mixture to warm up and stir.
3. Add the chunks in the pan and cook for 8 minutes, occasionally turning the chunks over. Add the rosemary. When done, remove the lobster chunks from the pan and maintain them warm in a large dish. Pour the sauce (the contents of the frying pan) in a food blender and blend for 1-2 minutes.
4. Pour the contents of the food mill (sauce) over lobster chunks in a large dish.

WINE & ROSEMARY MARINADE FOR VEAL AND LAMB

300 ml white wine
2 sprigs rosemary
4 tbsp olive oil
1 chilly pepper, small
2 cloves garlic, crushed

1. In a saucepan, boil the wine, pepper, garlic and rosemary for 10 minutes and then remove the saucepan from the heat.
2. Remove the chilly pepper and add the olive oil. Stir and let the marinade cool off. Immerse the meat in this mixture and place all in the fridge for 2-3 hours.

MINT

SOUP WITH YOGURT AND MINT

½ kg yogurt (strained)
4 tbsp extra virgin olive oil
1 clove garlic, crushed
1 large courgette, finely grated
1 tbsp fresh mint
2-3 drops of vinegar

1. Clean and grate the courgette. Salt and squeeze it by hand to drain its juice which you collect in a small bowl (do not dispose).
2. Whisk the yogurt in another, larger bowl for 5-6 minutes. Continue whisking while adding the vinegar, mint, courgette trims and its juice, garlic clove and olive oil. Continue whisking for 3-4 minutes. Place the soup in the fridge to chill.
3. Serve the soup cold in dishes with a cube of ice. Garnish with the chopped mint.

CYPRIOT GROATSALAD WITH SPEARMINT

Serves 8
½ cup of wheat grain or couscous
2 ripe tomatoes sliced in small cubs
1 spring onion, finely chopped
1 tbsp parsley, finely chopped
1 tsp spearmint, finely chopped
juice from a large ½ lemon
4 tbsp extra virgin olive oil
salt
pepper

1. Put the crushed grains/couscous in warm water and let them stand for 12 hours. Pick a handful of grains/couscous each time and squeeze to strain well. Place each handful in a salad bowl.
2. Add the tomatoes, spring onion, parsley, and spearmint. Add the salt, pepper, olive oil and lemon juice. Mix well with a spoon and serve as salad.

CHICKEN WITH RED PEPPERS AND SPEARMINT

Serves 6
1 medium size chicken in pieces
1 kg red, sweet peppers
3 spring onions, finely chopped
1 onion (bulb), finely chopped
½ tsp oregano
1 bunch spearmint
¾ cup olive oil
½ cup white wine, unresinated
salt
pepper

1. Wash the peppers and place them on the grill and switch to fan operation. Cook at 180ºC for 25-30 minutes.
2. Remove the peppers from the oven and place them in large dish and cover with transparent film (they puff out and are easily peeled).
3. Peel peppers, deseed, and set them aside on table.
4. Heat olive oil in non-stick casserole and gently stir-fry the onions turning them occasionally with a spoon. Add the chicken and brown them on both sides. Pour the wine over the chicken, add salt and pepper, add one and a half cup of water, cover pan and simmer for 35-40 minutes.
5. When chicken is done, remove from the heat, add the oregano, a tablespoon of mint finely chopped and stir. Empty the contents of the pan along with meat and sauce into a pyrex dish or similar fire-proof vessel and cover with lid. Stir in half the peppers. Make another bed of peppers on top. Cover and cook at 180ºC for 30-35 minutes in preheated oven.
6. Uncover and let peppers turn brown for 6-7 minutes. Serve chicken hot or at room temperature sprinkled with fresh *spearmint*.

The spicy spearmint and the sweet red pepper transform a simple piece of chicken into a luxurious and colorful dish.

SALTCOD WITH SAVORY AND MINT

Serves 6
1kg Saltcod fillets sliced in strips 4 cm wide
2 eggs, whisked
1 ½ cups ground toast
1 tbsp parsley, finely chopped
1 tbsp savory
1 tbsp mint, finely chopped
1 garlic clove, crushed
½ cup green olives, finely sliced
1 ½ cups olive oil (for frying only)
½ tsp freshly ground green pepper

1. Immerse codfish strips in cold water and let them rest for 8 hours to dissolve their salt, changing the water 4-5 times.
2. Dip codfish strips in the whisked eggs and then in the mixture of ground toast, garlic, parsley, pepper, savory, olives and mint.
3. Fry strips on both sides in hot oil for 6-7 minutes. When the codfish strips turn to a satisfactory brown colour, remove the frying pan from the oven ring and place the codfish on a large dish lined with kitchen paper to absorb oil. Serve immediately.

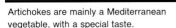

Artichokes are mainly a Mediterranean vegetable, with a special taste.

STUFFED ARTICHOKES WITH YOGURT SAUCE AND MINT

Serves 6
6 artichoke heads, fresh/canned/frozen
4 tbsp rice (used in stuffed vegetables)
1 ½ tbsp mint, finely chopped
3 spring onions, finely chopped
1 medium size onion bulb, finely ground
1 tbsp white wine, unresinated
7 tbsp yogurt (strained)
1 large egg
lemon juice, from a large lemon
1 cup olive oil
salt
green pepper, freshly ground

1. In a small saucepan heat the olive oil and sauté the spring onion for 2-3 minutes. Stir in the rice and add the wine. Add three tablespoons of water, cover the pan and simmer for 7 minutes. Stir in half the mint then turn off oven ring leaving the saucepan on to simmer for a while.
2. Peel the artichokes down to the very tender leaves. Crew-cut the remaining leaves and using a pointed knife remove the little mauve leaves and hair from the heart of the artichokes to form a cavity.

TZATZIKI WITH MINT

Serves 4
1 cup strained yogurt
2 cucumbers, grated
1 tsp fresh/dried mint or spearmint
3 cloves garlic, finely chopped
salt
2 drops vinegar
4 drops olive oil

1. Whisk the yogurt with the cucumbers, garlic, olive oil, salt and vinegar.
2. Pour the tzatziki in a bowl and sprinkle with mint. Chill the bowl for an hour before serving.

Toss the artichokes in a bowl with water where you have previously added the lemon juice and a teaspoon of salt.

3. Pull each artichoke out of the bowl, and rub them all over with a lemon cut in half. Fill each artichoke cavity with the mixture of rice.

4. Heat ½ cup of olive oil in a casserole and sauté the ground onion until it releases its juice, without getting brown. Place the artichokes in circular fashion at the bottom of the casserole, add a cup of water, cover and simmer for 12 minutes.

5. Transfer the artichokes with their juice to a small pyrex dish. Take a bowl and whisk the yogurt with the egg and a lot of green pepper. Pour this sauce over the artichokes and then cook in a preheated oven at 180ºC for 30 minutes.

6. Serve the artichokes hot with their sauce. Sprinkle with a lot of mint.

CHOCOLATE CAKE WITH MINT

Serves 12
2 cups sugar
1 3/4 cup all purpose flour, sifted
3/4 cup cocoa
1 tsp soda
1 tsp salt (not to the brim)

2 eggs
1 cup milk
½ cup extra virgin olive oil
2 drops vanilla essence
1 cup warm water
½ cup mint, finely chopped
1 tbsp butter (not completely full)
1 tbsp flour (to drizzle in cake tin)
1 tbsp icing sugar
mint leaves to garnish

1. Preheat the oven at 200ºC. Mix the sugar with the flour, cocoa, soda, salt, vanilla and mint in a large bowl.

2. In a second bowl mix the eggs (whisked) with milk, olive oil, and warm water.

3. Pour the contents of the second bowl into the first and process in a blender for 2-3 minutes and then manually for 6-7 minutes.

4. Choose a long cake tin and brush with butter, drizzle with flour and add in the cake mixture.

5. Bake at 180ºC for 40-45 minutes. Test the cake with the knife blade by stabbing it once or twice with the blade. If the blade comes out clean, then the cake is ready. When the cake is done, remove it from the oven and dust it with fine sugar. Serve the cake garnished with fresh mint.

Mint is a herb with many "privileges" as it can be used in both sweet and savory dishes. The spicy lemon taste goes well with chocolate, jams and citrus jellies.

PIES WITH SWEET PUMPKIN, RISE AND MINT

30 pieces
Stuffing:
2 cups of pumpkin flesh, sliced in cubes
2-3 tbsp rice
1 large onion (bulb)
4 tbsp olive oil
1 tbsp fresh mint, finely chopped
salt
pepper

Filo pastry sheet:
500 gr white flour
2 tbsp olive oil
2 tbsp lemon juice
salt
warm water for kneading

1. Slightly sauté the onion and pumpkin flesh in the olive oil. Add a little water, lower the heat and simmer for 15 minutes. Pick a fork and test if the pumpkin pieces are done. Press the pieces to mush them. Toss in the rice, mint, salt and pepper and continue simmering for 12 more minutes. Remove mixture from the oven ring and let it cool off completely.

2. With the filo pastry ingredients kneed a soft and elastic dough and divide into small balls. Roll out a long pastry sheet with each "ball" on a floured surface. Cut the filo into 7x7 cm squares and place a small quantity of filling in the middle of each square. Bring in the opposite corners of each

square together and press slightly in the middle to spread filling in the little pies. Place each pie in hot oil and fry until brown on both sides. Serve pies warm (not hot) or at room temperature.

REFRESHING ORANGE JELLY WITH MINT

Serves 6
1 kg oranges
2 tbsp sugar
1 box powdered orange gelatin
1 tbsp fresh mint, finely chopped

1. Wash and then dry oranges well with cotton cloth. Curve the orange skins longitudinally and peel oranges. Pick the orange skins and slice them longitudinally in 2 mm thin strips and let them dry well.

2. Squeeze an orange, collect its

juice in a small saucepan, and add two tablespoons of sugar. Place the saucepan on oven ring and bring the syrup to the boil. Then toss in the orange strips along with the mint. Lower heat to simmer for 5-6 minutes. Remove the orange strips with a perforated spoon and place them in a colander to drain.

3. Pick a shallow baking tin (plastic or metalic). Slice the peeled oranges in rings and layer them in the tin. Scatter the thin orange strips over the orange rings. Pour in the syrup and orange gelatin (dissolved in a glass of cold water).

4. Empty the syrup and gelatin in the tin. Place the tin in the refrigerator to chill for at least 8 hours and then serve.

MINT SAUCE

Serves 4
60 gr. fresh/dried
mint leaves,
ground
1 ½ cup vinegar
40 gr. sugar
salt
pepper

1. Bring vinegar to the boil and then pour it in a soup bowl with the mint leaves. Allow the vinegar to drop in temperature, until warm.

2. Add ½ glass of water, the sugar, salt and pepper. Stir well. This sauce is ideal for lamb dishes. Serve cold.

MINT MARMALADE WITH APPLES

100-200 gr mint leaves
1 kg apples, peeled and quartered
700 gr. sugar
2 lemons

1. Peel, quarter and toss the apples in ample cold water where you have previously added the lemon juice so that apples do not get dark. Let the apples stand in the water for a while, then strain and place them in saucepan, add the grated lemon rinds, mint (finely chopped), and a pinch of sugar.

2. Simmer, stir and skim until the apples are done. Remove the container from the heat and transfer the contents to a colander. You will get a green purée. To this add the sugar and the juice from the second lemon. Boil, stir and skim until the marmalade acquires a typical thickness.

3. Remove the saucepan from the heat and transfer the hot marmalade into small and airtight jars. Store the jars in a dark, cool place.

SAGE

FRIED SAGE LEAVES

Serves 10
The Batter
1 egg, the yolk
350 ml very chilled water
1/8 tsp soda
185 gr all purpose flour
30 large sage leaves

1. In a large metallic bowl mix all of the above ingredients, excepting the sage. Gently stir the ingredients with a wooden spoon to a watery mixture. Since this mixture looses its texture fast, pick the sage leaves and dip them in the batter and then into the frying pan with hot corn oil. This should not take more than 10 minutes. While frying, decide when the sage leaves are crispy enough to remove.

LARGE, LIMA BEANS WITH SAGE

Serves 6
500 gr large lima beans
6 cups of cold water
1/4 cup extra virgin olive oil
1 ½ tbsp sage, finely chopped
1 large clove garlic, crushed

1. Place the beans in a large pot. Add cold water to top beans by approximately 3 inches and let them soak overnight.
2. Strain the beans and place them back into the pot. Add the 6 cups of cold water, 1/4 cup of olive oil, sage (finely chopped) and garlic. Place the pot on oven ring at high temperature. On first boil, lower the temperature to moderate reading.
3. Cover the pot with lid and simmer for 45 min. or until the beans are tender. Occasionally stir the beans, then strain and sprinkle beans with the salt and pepper.
4. With a perforated spoon transfer the beans to a bowl. Pour the olive oil over the beans and garnish with fresh sage.

PORK RIBS WITH SAGE AND SWEET WINE

Serves 4
1 kg pork, shoulder (ribs side)
15 sage leaves

Two or three sage leaves are enough to take away the "earthy" taste of lima beans. When you cook with sage add it early on to starchy or mild-flavored ingredients such as grains and beans, to offset its strong flavour.

2 cloves garlic

the lemon juice from ½ lemon

1 bottle of sweet wine (700 ml)

½ cup olive oil

salt

pepper

1. Separate the ribs to 4 pieces and place them in a deep container with the lemon juice, olive oil, sweet wine, sage leaves (washed and

dried), and cloves of garlic (crushed). Add the salt, pepper and let them marinade.

2. Place the ribs on charcoal or on grill in preheated oven for 15 minutes making sure to turn ribs over for uniform cooking. Keep the ribs wet with the marinade, do not let them dry. Serve as soon as ribs are done.

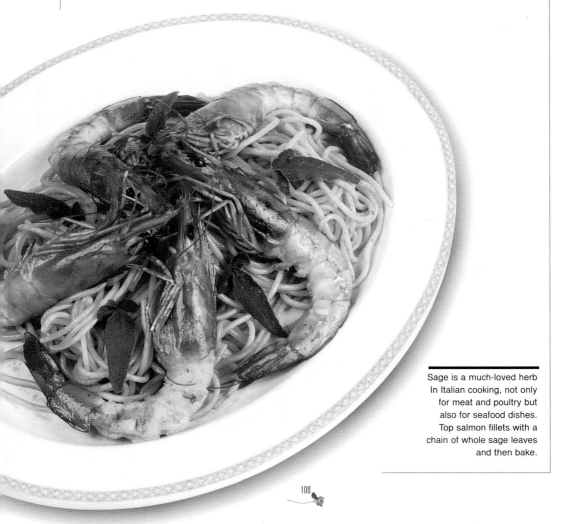

Sage is a much-loved herb In Italian cooking, not only for meat and poultry but also for seafood dishes. Top salmon fillets with a chain of whole sage leaves and then bake.

THYME

PORK WITH HONEY AND THYME

Serves 6
1 ½ kg baby pork, shoulder
side in medium size pieces
salt

Marinade:
2 ½ cups red wine
4 tbsp vinegar from red wine
4 tbsp thyme honey
2 tbsp thyme
1 bunch thyme, with sprigs
½ cup extra virgin olive oil
1 tsp salt
1 tsp green pepper

1. Rinse and dry the pork pieces well, and sprinkle with the salt. Place the pork in a large bowl and pour the marinade over. Marinade for at least 12 hours.
2. Scatter the thyme sprigs preferably in a large clay vessel. Arrange pork pieces on top of the sprigs and place the vessel in the oven at 200oC to bake for 20 minutes. Subsequently, open the oven window and pour a little marinade over the meat, lower heat to 180oC and continue cooking for another 20 minutes.
3. Again, open the oven window and pour ample marinade over the meat. Continue cooking for 20 more minutes. Make sure you turn meat over until it gets brown on all sides. Pour the rest of the marinade. Continue cooking for 25 more minutes.
4. Serve meat warm with its sauce. It marries well with green salad.

SOUP WITH SHRIMPS AND THYME

Serves 6
800 gr potatoes
300 gr shrimps, with heads
1/4 cup extra virgin olive oil
1 sprig celery, finely chopped
1 carrot, finely chopped
2 spring onions, finely chopped
3 sprigs thyme
1 cup dry white wine
1/3 cup fresh cream
salt
pepper
1 tbsp butter
parsley

1. Preheat oven at 250oC. Wrap each potato in foil and cook for approximately 50 minutes. Rinse the potatoes under tap water to cool, then peel the and set them aside.
2. Remove, but save the heads, shrimp shells and tails. Sauté the heads, shells, tails in the olive oil, along with the parsley, carrot, onions and

thyme. Add the wine and let it evaporate. Then add 6 ups of water. Cover the container and cook at moderate heat for 10 minutes.

3. Strain and collect the juice. Blender the potatoes along with 5 cups of the stock. Add the fresh cream, salt and pepper and allow the mixture to simmer at low heat to produce a tasty soup.

4. Cut the shrimps in two; sauté them in butter, salt and pepper them. Serve the soup garnished with the shrimps and basil.

PENNE WITH MARJORAM

Serves 6
1 packet of penne (500 gr)
4 tender artichokes (peeled, cleaned and cut to slices of 4-5 mm and sprinkled with lemon juice)
3 tbsp white wine
1 onion, finely sliced
1 garlic clove, finely sliced
½ cup olive oil
½ tsp sugar
½ tsp dried basil
½ tsp thyme
3 ripe tomatoes, peeled and cut in cubes
3 tbsp parmesan or pecorino, grated

1. Put the artichokes, onion, garlic, sugar, thyme, basil, wine and 8 tablespoons of water in a large non-stick frying pan. Steam them by shaking the frying pan back-and-forth; do not stir,

otherwise artichokes may dissolve. When the juice has evaporated, add the olive oil and sauté.

2. Add the tomatoes, pepper, then turn off oven ring (Mark 0) and cover the frying pan.

3. Boil the pasta in water and, when done, strain, but keep one cup of water. Mix the pasta with the sauce, the water you kept, and transfer all to a large dish. Sprinkle with sweet cheese ("myzithra") and serve immediately.

PIE WITH OLIVES, DRIED TOMATOES AND THYME

Serves 10
½ kg white self-rising flour
½ kg corn flour
1 cup olives (Kalamata or other "pickled" type), finely sliced
1 cup tomatoes, dried and finely chopped
½ cup dried oregano, finely chopped
½ tsp dried thyme
½ tsp sugar
1 tbsp fresh parsley
½ tsp sugar
½ tsp salt
3 eggs
½ cup olive oil
2 cups orange juice
3 baking powder

white sesame
nigella seeds

1.   In a large bowl mix the olive oil, orange juice, the herbs, eggs (whisked), parsley, salt, pepper and sugar. Stir all to mix well.
2.   Mix the flour with the baking powder and slowly pour this mixture in the bowl but keep stirring with the other hand. Flour the olives and tomatoes well and add them to the mixture. Add the remaining flour until you get a firm and homogenous mixture (not too firm, but more like dough for cake).
3.   Slightly oil a fairly deep baking pan and drizzle its bottom with corn flour; pour in the mixture and sprinkle with white and black sesame. Bake at 180ºC for one hour approximately. Cut pie as soon as cool.

OLIVE OIL SCENTED WITH THYME AND GREEN LEMON / LIME

1 cup extra virgin olive oil
the skin/rind of 1 green lemon or lime
(coiled skin/rind)
4 sprigs thyme
1 skewer stick
1 bottle

1.   Pierce the lemon skin/rind with skewer stick.
2.   Insert in sterilized bottle the thyme sprigs and the skewer with lemon/lime skin/rind.
3.   Fill the bottle with extra virgin olive oil and seal.

LAUREL

PICKLING ONIONS IN VINEGAR

2 kg pickling onions
1 kg white vinegar
100 gr. sugar
a few basil leaves
4 laurel leaves
salt
6-7 black pepper corns

1. Peel the onions and immerse
    them in warm salted-water (containing a few tablespoons of
    vinegar) for 3 minutes. Subsequently, remove, wipe dry, and
    place the onions in jars; slightly pressing each to fit in jars
    well.
2. Mix the vinegar with the sugar,
    basil and laurel and place them on heat to come to the boil.
    Strain the mixture and pour it in the jars.
3. Add a few pepper corns and
    fresh basil leaves in each jar. Seal jars tightly and store in a
    cool, dark place.

Choose a suitable container to accommodate
the desired quantity of milk.
Add one or two laurel leaves in the milk
and warm up – do not boil.
You can use this milk scented thus
to make puddings, cream caramel, or cream broule.

Laurel gives a special taste to pickles and conserves.
Do not forget that fresh laurel is more potent than dried.

PAPPARDELLE WITH RABBIT AND LAUREL

Serves 8
1 whole rabbit in pieces
½ cup olive oil
a little flour
1 large onion, finely sliced
2 carrot sticks sliced 1 cm thick
2 celery sticks, finely sliced
½ cup red wine
1 cup white wine
3 tbsp fresh cream
1 packet pappardelle

For the marinade:
1 ½ cup brandy
1 tbsp vinegar
1 tbsp sugar
2 cloves garlic
a few rosemary leaves
3 laurel leaves
2 tbsp dried thyme
salt
pepper
1 cup of water (for cooking)

1. Place the rabbit pieces in the marinade and refrigerate for 24 hours (3 hours for the rabbit). Then dispose the marinade and flour the rabbit.
2. Pick a large casserole, add the olive oil and gently sauté the meat in portions. Then remove the meat and stir-fry in the same olive oil the onion, carrot and celery. Return the meat into the casserole and add the wine. Add 6-8 cups of water and simmer for 40-50 minutes until the meat is very tender.
3. Remove the meat from the casserole making sure that no bones are left behind, and cook the sauce until it is thick Now, remove the bones by shredding the meat in small pieces. Transfer the sauce to a blender, process it to pulp and return it to the casserole and stir continually. As soon as the sauce comes to a boil add the cream and shredded rabbit pieces. Turn off (Mark 0) heat.
4. Boil the pappardelle for 4 minutes, strain, and place them in a large warm dish and mix with half the sauce. Then pour the remaining sauce over the pappardele and serve immediately.

MARJORAM

GREEK PANCAKES WITH OLIVES AND MARJORAM

1 ½ cups of extra virgin olive oil
3-4 cups of tepid water
½ kg self-rising flour
½ cup black olives, deseeded and halved
½ cup green olives, deseeded and halved
1 medium size onion, finely chopped
1 tsp marjoram, finely chopped
salt
pepper

1. Pick a large bowl to mix the herbs, olives, salt and pepper. Add the flour and mix well working manually. Pour in the tepid water slowly until the mixture turns moderately pulpy.
2. Warm the olive oil in a frying pan and add the mixture spoon-by-spoon. Turn the "pancakes" over to brown on both sides. Then remove and place them on large dish covered with kitchen paper to absorb the remaining oil on them. You can serve them warm or cold.

LITTLE PIES WITH CHEESE AND MARJORAM

For 10-12 pies
300 gr. flour
130 gr butter
1 egg
4 thin slices ham
1 small red onion
300 gr fresh goat cheese
8 small marjoram leaves
4 small tomatoes
extra virgin olive oil
salt

1. Pour in a mixer small quantities of the flour, butter (soft), and egg; add a pinch of salt and ½ lt of cold water and process until the mixture turns to homogenous dough. Wrap dough in foil and let it rest for 30 minutes in the refrigerator. Repeat the procedure with the rest of the ingredients.
2. Chop the onion and sauté for 10 minutes in 2 tablespoons of olive oil and 2 tablespoons of water. Add the ham strips, raise the heat and cook for 3-4 minutes. Pick dough 2-3 mm thick and line the non-stick tart tin moulds (12 cm diametre). Pierce the bottom of the moulds with a fork, and put in moulds equal portions of onion, ham and cheese. Sprinkle with a little salt, add the marjoram leaves and tomato slices
3. Bake the tarts in the oven at 180ºC for 20-25 minutes. Serve warm or cold.

FENNEL

PASTA SHELLS WITH LOBSTER AND FENNEL

Serves 6
1 packet of pasta shells
1 large lobster
½ cup olive oil
2 tbsp fennel, finely chopped
1 large onion, finely chopped
1 cup wine, unresinated
1 tbsp tomato paste
1 laurel leaf
1 fresh and ripe tomato, finely chopped
salt
freshly ground black pepper

1. Rinse the lobster well under tap water and cut it in fairly large pieces. Heat the olive oil in a large pot and sauté the lobster for 4-5 minutes, then pour wine over.
2. Add the laurel leaf, tomato pulp, fresh tomato slices and 4-5 cups of water. Cover the pot with lid and cook in moderate heat for 15-20 minutes.
3. Add the pasta shells, fennel, salt and a little pepper. Stir and simmer for 10 more minutes. Serve as soon as done.

MUSSELS WITH WINE AND FENNEL SEEDS

Serves 6
60 mussels with shells
1 large onion, finely chopped
350 ml of dry white wine
2 tbsp olive oil
1 ½ tbsp flour
2 tbsp fennel seeds
½ tsp nutmeg
little salt
3-4 green pepper corns, freshly ground

1. Brush the mussels and rinse well to remove any grit. Scrape shells with knife, if

necessary, to remove anything attached on them.
2. Steam mussels in a large pot for 6 minutes. Take the pot off the heat, remove and dispose one-half of the shell and place the other half with its content in a large dish and keep them warm.
3. Sauté the onion in a second pot with the olive oil and add

A most interesting combination of the Cretan cuisine: fresh spinach and fennel braised with cuttlefish.

the wine. Add the fennel seeds, salt, nutmeg and let all simmer for 8 minutes. Dissolve flour in a little glass of wine and pour its contents in the sauce and stir well. Pour sauce over hot mussels and sprinkle with freshly ground green pepper.

SPICED OLIVE OIL WITH GINGER AND FENNEL SEEDS

*1 thick ginger piece, approx. 3 cm /
1 ½ inch
2 tsp fennel seeds
1 cup olive oil
1 empty bottle (225 ml)*

1. Cut the ginger in thin slices. Gently crush the fennel seeds in mortar.
2. Insert the herbs in the empty bottle and pour in the olive oil. Seal the bottle.
3. Two (2) weeks later remove the herbs from the bottle.

CUTTLEFISH WITH FENNEL AND SPINACH

*Serves 6
1 kg cuttlefish
1 cup fennel
2 cups chopped spinach
2 spring onions
1 small onion, finely sliced
1 medium size tomato, cubed
the juice from 1 large lemon
1 cup olive oil
salt
pepper*

1. Clean and rinse the cuttlefish well.
2. Pick a large heavy-bottom pot and heat the olive oil. Stir-fry the onion for 1-2 minutes then add the cuttlefish to brown on both sides. Add 3 cups of water, cover pot with lid and simmer for at least 40-45 minutes.
3. Add the spinach, fennel, spring onions, tomato, salt, pepper and, if required, a little water. Cove pot with lid and continue cooking at low temperature unit the greens are soft.
4. Pour the lemon juice and stir well. Let the meal rest for 10-15 minutes before you serve.

SAFFRON

PASTRIES WITH CHEESE AND SAFFRON

240 gr. butter milk
160 gr granulated sugar
2 eggs
4 cups flour

Filling:
1 kg ricotta or other
sweet and soft
cheese
2-3 saffron stamens,
dissolved in slightly
warm water
1 egg
3 tbsp granulated sugar
1 egg yolk (for brushing)
cinnamon

1. In a mixer process the butter and sugar at medium speed for 3 minutes. Slowly add the eggs and flour until the mixture turns into a very soft dough. Slightly butter a few moulds (4cm high) and line them with the dough.
2. Fill the moulds with the mixture of sweet cheese. Brush the top of the mixture with the egg yolk, dust with a little cinnamon and bake in preheated oven at 180°C for 30 minutes.
3. Let the cakes cool and then remove the moulds. Serve cakes cool.

PAPPARDELLE WITH SAFFRON

Serves 6
400 gr. pappardelle
20 gr onion, finely chopped
1 clove garlic
$^1/_4$ tsp sweet paprika
2 tomatoes, finely chopped
$^3/_4$ tbsp dry white wine
1 cup chicken stock
granulated sugar, just a bit at the tip of a teaspoon
1 cup grouvier, grated
olive oil
salt

1. In a heavy bottom non-stick frying pan, stir-fry the garlic, paprika, and onion.
2. When the garlic begins to brown a little, remove it and add the tomatoes. Continue stir-frying until the tomatoes are soft and add the wine. Cover the frying pan with lid and simmer for 5 minutes.
3. Boil the pappardelle in ample salted water for 4-5 minutes, where you have previously added the saffron. Remove and serve the pappardelle in a large dish. Pour the sauce over and sprinkle with ample cheese.

ROSE

MARZIPAN WITH ROSE

40 pieces
2 egg whites
1 egg, the yolk
600 gr. granulated sugar
the juice from one small lemon
2-3 drops bitter almond essence
3 drops rose-water
1 kg almonds, cleaned and ground
1-2 tbsp breadcrumbs
2 cups icing sugar

1. In a bowl or mixer bring to meringue the albumen, sugar and a few drops of lemon juice.
2. Add the yolk, almonds and essence of bitter almond and mix gently to produce the dough. If the dough is watery, add a little of the breadcrumbs. Pick a little dough and kneed round buns to produce the marzipan
3. Place the marzipan in a large baking pan lined with baking sheet. Bake at 200°C for 15 minutes. When the marzipans are slightly brown, remove them from the oven and drizzle them with rose-water immediately. When done, sprinkle marzipans with icing sugar.

ROSE-VINEGAR FROM ROSE PETALS

1 kg vinegar
80 gr. rose petals from scented roses

1. Harvest the roses early in the morning. Wash the petals and remove the anthers, the point where the petals join the stamen. Mix the petals in the vinegar.
2. Let the petals ferment for 10 days, then strain the vinegar in a bottle.
3. This juice is used to sprinkle over potato salad.

Greek yogurt served with rose petal jam.

POPPIES

BREAD WITH POPPY SEEDS

1 ½ kg white flour
2 cups granulated sugar
6 tbsp fresh butter at room
temperature
2 tbsp olive oil
1 tsp salt
5 eggs
½ tbsp cinnamon, ground
45 gr. fresh yeast
2 tbsp milk
2 tbsp poppy seeds

1. In a mixer bowl add the olive oil, the butter, sugar and yeast (dissolved in warm water). Operate the mixer for two minutes at a low speed. Add the 4 eggs, cinnamon, salt and continue with the mixer for 3 more minutes at same speed. Work for 8 more minutes slowly adding the rest of the flour and making sure that the dough is to your satisfaction. The dough should then be soft and pliable. If necessary, add a little warm water or a little flour.

2. Next, transfer the dough to a large bowl, cover with a cotton cloth and let it rest for 45 minutes. The dough should then have risen to almost double in size. Place dough on smooth, slightly floured surface and divide it into pieces with respect to the size of loaves you intend to produce.

3. Place the loaves in a large baking pan, but previously brush pan with olive oil. Cover loaves with a cotton cloth and allow them 30 minutes to rise. Preheat oven at 200ºC for 8 minutes, whisk an egg and mix with the milk. Use this mixture to brush the surface of each loaf. Sprinkle with ample poppy seeds and bake in moderate temperature for 50 minutes, until each loaf becomes golden brown in colour.

PIQUANT CARROT-CAKE WITH POPPY SEEDS

1 cup honey
½ cup olive oil
½ cup margarine
250 gr. ground carrots
1 tsp grated orange rind

1 cup yogurt
2 eggs, whisked
1 ½ tbsp poppy seeds
1 tsp cinnamon
1 tsp carnation, ground
3 tbsp currant, soaked in water
170-180 gr. rising flour
1 tsp baking powder

1. Preheat oven at 180ºC.
   Slightly butter a round cake tin (20 cm. diam.).
2. Pick a large bowl and add the olive oil, margarine and honey. Mix well until all ingredients turn into a homogenous thin pulp. Add the yogurt, spices, eggs, grated orange rind and continue working manually or in the mixer bowl to produce a "watery" mixture.
3. Mix the flour with the baking powder. Toss in the "watery" mixture the currants (strained) and the poppy seeds. Also, slowly add the flour–baking powder mixture. Work vigorously so that they mix well. Empty the contents of the bowl in the cake tin, even its surface with a spatula and bake at 200ºC for 10 minutes. Lower heat to 180ºC and bake for 20 more minutes. When the cake is done, let it cool off and then cut it to slices.

FIG

DESERT WITH FRESH FIGS AND FILO PASTRY SHEETS

Serves 10
6 fresh, large figs, cleaned and
chopped into pieces
2 tbsp sugar, brown
2 tbsp walnuts

heat and stir in the walnuts and spices. Let the mixture cool off completely.

2. Place the filo sheet on a flat surface and brush it with butter. Place the next sheet over the first, butter again and repeat the procedure with the remaining filo sheets.

3. Spoon the mixture over the top layer and roll them in. Place them on a baking pan, brush them with butter and bake them at 180oC for 45 minutes.

4. When done, remove them from the oven, sprinkle with icing sugar, cut in pieces and serve.

1 tbsp raisins
½ tsp cinnamon
1 mastic piece, crushed
1 tbsp brandy
7 filo pastry sheets
sugar icing (to sprinkle)

1. Preheat oven at 180oC. Put the figs, brandy, raisins and sugar in casserole dish with a tablespoon of water. Cover the casserole with lid and simmer for 5 minutes. Remove casserole from the

ASPARAGUS

ASPARAGUS WITH SESAME

Serves 6
500 gr green asparagus
1 tbsp butter
4 spring onions, finely chopped
½ tsp lemon skin, grated
1 tbsp lemon juice
1 tbsp sesame, slightly roasted
salt
black pepper, freshly ground

1.   Peel and rinse the asparagus under running water.
2.   Remove the hard part of the stem and slice the asparagus in small pieces. Place the pieces in a pot with salted water. Boil for 8-10 minutes until they turn quite tender.
3.   Pick a large, heavy bottom frying-pan, heat the butter to melt and add the spring onions. Stir-fry for one minute and then add the juice, the grated lemon rind and asparagus pieces.
4.   Gently stir-fry the asparagus for 3 more minutes before you add the salt and pepper.
5.   When done, place the asparagus in a warm dish and sprinkle with ample sesame.

ASPARAGUS TART WITH GREEN OLIVES

Tart tin of 25 cm. diam.
3 eggs
280 ml fresh cream
½ tsp salt
1 pinch of nutmeg
freshly ground pepper
1 tbsp flour
298 gr. fresh green asparagus
90 gr. green olives
1 onion, finely chopped
1 tbsp butter
45 gr cheddar cheese, grated
1 tbsp grated parmesan
30 gr butter

1.   Preheat oven at 200ºC. Whisk the eggs with the cream and add the salt, nutmeg and pepper. Take a little portion of the mixture and mix it with the flour to make a thin paste and then add it back to the previous mixture.
2.   Arrange the asparagus pieces and olives in the tart mould. Sauté the onions in butter until tender then pour this over the asparagus and olives. Over this pour the fresh cream mixture. Sprinkle with ground cheddar cheese, parmesan and melted butter (30gr) and bake for 25 minutes.
3.   Lower heat to 180ºC and bake for 15 more minutes until the surface of the cake turns golden brown.

Crisp asparagus flavored with fresh butter and sprinkled with healthy tasty sesame, laid on a bed of red tomatoes.

ROCKET

LETTUCE AND ROCKET SALAD

4-5 lettuce hearts
20 fresh broad beans
1 bunch rocket
1 tsp finely chopped dill
salt

for the sauce:
4 tbsp olive oil
2 tbsp vinegar (from wine)
1 clove garlic, crushed
salt
pepper

1.   Rinse the lettuce and rocket well and let them dry completely before using.
2.   Over a large bowl cut the lettuce and rocket to pieces by hand. Separately skin and salt the beans and then toss them in the salad bowl.
3.   Pour the olive oil, vinegar, crushed garlic, salt, pepper and a tablespoon of warm water in a glass jar that seals well. Shake the mixture vigorously to make a thick juice. This juice is now your salad dressing. Garnish the salad with dill and serve.

WHEAT SALAD WITH PEAS, ROCKET AND TOMATOES

Serves 8
6 cups of water
2 cups of wheat
5 tbsp olive oil
2 ½ tbsp vinegar (from red wine)
1 cup fresh/frozen peas
2 cups fresh rocket leaves, cut in half
3 tomatoes, deseeded and finely chopped
rocket leaves

1.   In a medium size casserole pour the 6 cups of water and add the wheat. As soon as they come to a boil, lower heat to medium range. Half-cover the casserole with a lid and let the wheat simmer until tender (approx. 45 minutes). Then strain the wheat and transfer it to a large bowl. Mix the olive oil with vinegar in a large bowl and add the salt. Pour this mixture over wheat and place the bowl with the wheat in the refrigerator.
2.   Boil the peas until tender. Strain and place peas in a bowl with chilled water for 1 minute. Strain the peas again. Add the peas to the wheat, cover and refrigerate.
3.   Add the rocket and tomatoes in the wheat-peas mixture and stir well. Add enough salt and transfer the salad into a salad bowl. Garnish with the rocket leaves.

Wheat, rocket, peas, tomatoes and olive oil: a dish amulating the ancient Greek and Roman cuisine.

CHICORY

CHICORY WITH LAMB AND CORIANDER

Serves 6
1 kg wild chicory, finely chopped
1 kg lamb (shoulder blade) in pieces
2 onions, finely sliced
2 large ripe tomatoes, finely chopped
3/4 cup olive oil
1 tsp dried coriander
4 seeds of pimento
salt
pepper, freshly ground (as much as you prefer)

1. Stir-fry the onions in the olive oil until slightly roasted. Add the meat in slices. Continue stir-frying until the lamb pieces acquire a golden-brown colour. Add the salt, coriander, pimento and two cups of water. Stir well and cover the container to simmer for 40 minutes approximately.
2. Pick a little meat with fork to taste it. When the meat is almost done, add the chicory, tomatoes, a little water and stir. Continue cooking for 20-30 more minutes.
3. Sprinkle with freshly ground pepper and serve while the meal is still warm.

CASSEROLE CHICORY

Serves 6
1 kg chicory
3 large onions, finely chopped
½ cup olive oil
3 tomatoes, finely sliced
4 tbsp vinegar
little sugar
little salt
pepper, freshly ground (at will)

1. Stir-fry the onions in olive oil until slightly golden. Add the chicory, tomatoes, sugar, salt, vinegar and two cups of water. Taste to see if the chicory is tender enough and add a little vinegar, if necessary.
2. Serve this meal warm with ample freshly ground pepper.

NETTLE

NETTLE SPIRAL PIES

20 pies
1 kg nettles
3 spring onions
½ cup black vinegary olive oils,
deseeded and finely chopped
½ cup walnuts, crushed
4 cups olive oil (for frying)
little cumin
salt
pepper
for the pastry sheet:
2 cups flour
1 tbsp vodka
4 tbsp olive oil
1 cup lukewarm water
salt

1. Clean and rinse the nettles well under running water.
2. Strain well and sauté nettles in a deep pan with the onions in 5 tablespoons of olive oil for 5 minutes. Add the olives, walnuts, cumin, salt and pepper. Test to see if the cumin and pepper are to your liking. Add more if required.
3. Pastry sheet preparation: mix the vodka with olive oil, salt, a little flour and a little lukewarm water. Process at low speed for 10 minutes and gradually add the flour. Occasionally stop processing to check if the dough holds together. If the dough is runny, add a little flour, then check again. Stop processing if the dough is to your satisfaction.
4. On a slightly floured board roll out the dough and cut in rectangular strips of 7 cm wide and 30 cm long. Spoon in a little of the filling along each strip and bring the long sides together to close the strips. Hold one end of the filled strip and roll it in to form a spiral.
5. Preheat ample olive oil in a frying pan and fry the nettle pies. Sever them warm

NETTLE SOUP

1 kg nettles
1 spring onion, chopped to pieces
1 medium size onion, finely grated
1 large potato, boiled
4 tbsp olive oil
1 tbsp (not full) fresh butter
3 cups chicken stock
1 cup milk
a few leaves of fresh mint
salt
pepper

1.   Using gloves clean and wash the nettles under running water. Boil them for 17 minutes and pull them from pot using perforated spoon. Let them strain well.
2.   Sauté the onions in a casserole with butter until the onions are tender enough but not brown. Add the olive oil, potato, stock and boil for 20 minutes.
3.   Cut the boiled potato and process the pieces in a food processor along with the nettles. Transfer to nettle pulp back to the casserole, add the milk and stir vigorously. Taste to see if more salt and/or pepper is required.
4.   Serve the soup warm, garnished with mint leaves.

FENNEL SOUP WITH NETTLES

1 kg nettles roughly cut
1 bunch fennel, only the tender part
1 large onion, grated
½ cup olive oil
1 handful of white short grain rice
the juice from one lemon
salt
pepper

1.   Immerse the nettles in boiling water and boil for 3 minutes. Finely chop and then rub the other greens between your hands over a bowl.
2.   Stir-fry the onions in olive oil until slightly brown. Add the other greens: the nettles (strained) and fennel. Sauté for 8 minutes at low temperature.
3.   Add a little salt, pepper and 5 cups of water. Boil the soup for 10 minutes. Add the rice, lower the heat and cook the soup for 12 more minutes.
4.   Taste the soup and make the necessary adjustments with salt and pepper. Add the lemon juice and serve immediately.

CAPER

FUSILLI WITH TUNA, CAPERS AND LEMON

Serves 6
1 packet fusilli (spring-shaped pasta)
tuna fish in water, 1 can
½ cup extra virgin olive oil
1 tbsp caper
2 fillets anchovies
1 tsp parsley, finely chopped
1 tsp fresh basil, finely chopped
1 tsp grated lemon rinds
3-4 drops of lemon juice

1. Mash the anchovies in a bowl with a fork and slowly drop and stir in the olive oil until the anchovies turn into a pulp.
2. Strain the tuna fish chunks and toss them in the bowl. "Crack" the chunks with the fork and sprinkle the parsley, basil, and 3-4 drops of lemon juice and the capers.
3. Boil the pasta in ample salted water, strain and transfer it to a large bowl. Pour the sauce over the pasta and stir vigorously using two forks. Sprinkle with the grated lemon rind and parmesan cheese (optional).
4. Serve immediately.

CHICKEN JELLY WITH CAPER

Serves 8
1 medium size chicken, sliced in pieces
2 hard boiled eggs
1 ½ tbsp fine caper
3-4 gherkin pickles, roughly sliced
the juice from 2 lemons
salt
seeds of green pepper
black pepper, finely ground
4-5 gelatins

1. Boil the chicken pieces well in a pot with salted water at medium heat. The pot should be covered with a lid.
2. When the chicken pieces are done, pull them out with a strainer-spoon and set them aside to cool off. Strain the stock through a fine sieve. Let the stock cool off completely (it is best to store it in the fridge for 40 minutes), it is then much easier to scoop off the surfaced fat.
3. Remove the skin and bones from the chicken and cut its flesh to little pieces. Place flesh in wide and shallow bowl or long baking tin. Sprinkle with the peppers, salt, caper, and pickles. Arrange the sliced eggs on top.
4. Immerse the gelatins in a cup of tepid chicken stock to melt.

Then vigorously stir this mixture in the remaining cool stock and pour over the chicken and eggs.

5. Place the meal in the refrigerator for 8-10 hours before carving and serving.

ORECCHIETTE WITH CAPERS, ROSEMARY AND DRIED TOMATOES

Serves 6
1 packet of orecchiette (ear-shaped pasta)
1 tbsp salted caper
½ cup olive oil
2 clovers garlic, crushed
4 dried tomatoes, conserved in olive oil
1 small chilly pepper (cut in two)
1 sprig of rosemary
20 gr. pine seeds
black pepper, freshly ground
salt
ground parmesan cheese

1. Let the capers rest in cold, clear water for 1-2 hours, then rinse and set it aside.
2. Slightly stir-fry the onions in the olive oil for 1-2 minutes, add the tomatoes, stir in the hot pepper, pine seeds, rosemary and capers.
3. Boil the ear-shaped pasta in ample salted water, strain and transfer it in a large flat dish. Pour the sauce over the pasta and stir vigorously. Serve with ample ground pepper and grated cheese.

POTATO SALAD WITH CAPERS AND MINT

Serves 6
5 medium size potatoes
1 large onion, roughly sliced
1 tbsp capers
1 tsp mint, finely chopped
5-6 black olives, salted
½ cup extra virgin olive oil
salt
black pepper, freshly ground
2 tbsp vinegar, from red wine

1. Wash the potatoes under running water and boil them in ample water for 30 minutes. Do not clean them first. Let them cool off first, then peel and cut in fairly large pieces.
2. Place the potato pieces in a large bowl and add in the onion, capers, mint, a little salt, and stir well with two spoons. Pick a glass jar and pour in the olive oil, vinegar, a little salt and two drops of tepid water. Seal the jar well and shake the mixture well to mix all ingredients.
3. Pour the mixture over the potato salad, sprinkle with a little pepper and serve.

Wild capers growing on a wall at the Chrisoskalitisa monastery in Chania. They remind us of white summer roses.

Cleaning fresh capers on the island of Tinos.

EGGS STUFFED WITH BREAD AND CAPERS

Serves 6
6 eggs
4 tbsp butter
2 tbsp mustard
1 tbsp mayonnaise
1 tbsp capers
salt
pepper

1. Hard-boil the eggs in slightly vinegary and salted water for 15-20 minutes.
2. Shell, halve the eggs, and remove the yolks. Mush the yolks with a fork and add the butter, mayonnaise, mustard, capers and salt. Mix them well and fill in the egg-halves with the mixture.
3. Sprinkle filled egg-halves with pepper; place them in the refrigerator for 30 minutes and then serve.

1. Rinse the fish fillets well and tap them dry with kitchen paper.
2. Put the capers in a bowl and rinse well with ample running water. Strain the capers and toss them in a clean bowl. Add the breadcrumbs, parsley, half the butter quantity (iced and in cube form), salt and pepper.
3. Mix well and spread the mixture on the fillet surfaces. Roll in the fillets starting from the wide end and pierce to hold rolls with 2 toothpicks.
4. Arrange the fish-fillet rolls in fire-proof casserole, salt, pepper, and sprinkle the remaining butter cubes and fresh cream over the fillets. Cook at 200ºC for 30-40 minutes until you get a golden crust.

STUFFED SOLE FILLETS WITH CAPERS

Serves 6
6 sole fillets
1 cup fine capers in vinegar
4 tbsp fresh butter
1 bunch of parsley, finely chopped
1 cup breadcrumbs
1 fresh cream, 250 ml
salt
pepper

CAPER SAUCE

Serves 4
50 gr flour
1 tbsp ground capers
seasoned with vinegar
1 tbsp whole capers
seasoned with vinegar
1 tbsp butter
1 tbsp vinegar

1. Warm ½ lt of water in a container and stir in one tablespoon of butter to melt in low temperature. Add the flour and stir well to prevent lumps.

2. Cook for two more minutes and slowly add warm water stirring continually. Then add one tablespoon of vinegar and all the capers.

3. Cover the container and simmer for 30 minutes. Turn oven ring off (Mark 0) and leave the covered saucepan on ring for 15 more minutes before serving.

Sun dried tomatoes, capers and rosemary with pasta.

POMEGRANATE

LEGUME SALAD WITH WHEAT AND POMEGRANATE

Serves 6
½ cup black eyed beans
½ cup small, white beans
½ cup broad beans
½ cup chickpeas
1 cup wheat, boiled
1 cup pomegranate seeds
3 tbsp olive oil
1 tbsp vinegar
salt

1. Put the white beans, broad beans and chickpeas in separate bowls, top them with water and let them soak for 8 hours. Boil the legumes in separate pots, then rinse them under running water and strain well. Mix all legumes in a larger bowl and stir in the wheat, olive oil, salt, and vinegar.
2. Empty the contents of the bowl in a large dish, let them cool off and garnish with the pomegranate seeds.

CRETAN SALAD WITH GREENS AND POMEGRNATE MOLASSES

Serves 6
½ kg bitter chicory, finely chopped
2 cups endives, finely chopped
1 tbsp leeks, finely chopped
2 spring onions, finely sliced
1 tsp fresh mint
2 tbsp virgin olive oil
4 tbsp pomegranate molasses
salt

Clean and rinse the greens under running water. Let them strain well; chop them well and toss all in a large bowl. Drizzle with the olive oil, pour the molasses and serve.

POMEGRANATE MOLASSES

20 very ripe pomegranates
½ cup granulated sugar
½ cup lemon juice

1. Carve each pomegranate crosswise from top to bottom and crack it carefully into four pieces. Separate the seeds from the skin and place the seeds in a large bowl.
2. Pick a handful of seeds, place them in clean cotton kerchief, gently squeeze and catch the juice in a bowl. Repeat the procedure with the remaining of the pomegranate seeds.
3. Transfer the juice in a saucepan and add the sugar and lemon juice. Boil at high temperature until the contents of the saucepan can fill approximately 1 ½ cups. Let the syrup cool off and then transfer it to glass jars. Keep it refrigerated for more than a year.

Mixed pulses with pomegranate seeds: a traditional offering to God to entreat fertility of land.

BORAGE

REFRESHING BORAGE SALAD WITH CUCUMBER

1/4 cup sweet soft cheese (sweet "myzithra")

6 tbsp yogurt (strained)

2 tbsp blanched almonds, finely chopped

1 tbsp cucumber, finely chopped

1 cup fresh borage leaves and shoots, finely chopped

1 tbsp lemon juice

2 tbsp olive oil

salt

20 borage flowers (to garnish)

1. Spoon in the sweet cheese, yogurt, olive oil, and lemon juice in a food processor and process for 3 minutes.

2. Add the almonds, cucumber, borage, salt and gently stir with wooden spoon to mix all ingredients well.

3. Test the salad and correct the taste with a little salt or lemon, if necessary. Fill in a few glass bowls with this salad. Let them chill in the refrigerator and garnish with borage leaves before serving.

Refreshing borage salad with cucumber and almonds.

PURSLANE

CHICKEN WITH PURSLANE

Serves 6
1 kg purslane
1 kg baby courgettes
1 chicken, sliced
2 potatoes, quartered
2-3 fresh tomatoes, finely chopped
1 large onion, finely chopped
½ cup red wine
1 cup olive oil
salt
black pepper, freshly ground

1. Sauté the chicken pieces and onion in olive oil until slightly golden on all sides. Add the wine, two cups of water, cover the casserole and simmer for 35 minutes.
2. Add the potatoes and a little water (if necessary) and continue cooking for 15 more minutes with casserole covered.
3. Add the courgettes, purslane, tomatoes, salt, pepper and gently shake the casserole to mix ingredients with chicken. Simmer for 25-30 minutes until you get a thick sauce. Serve the meal warm or cold.

MISCELLANEOUS

TURKEY WITH HERBS

Serves 12
1 turkey of 3 kg
1 tbsp fresh rosemary
1 tbsp thyme
1 tbsp savory
1 tsp fresh marjoram
1 small bunch of mixed herbs (sage, rosemary and thyme)
1 tsp green peppers
3 tbsp olive oil
3 tbsp fresh butter
2 tsp coarse grain sea salt
½ kg chicken wings

for the sauce:
½ cup brandy
2 tbsp butter
½ cup all purpose flour
4 cups chicken stock
2 tbsp fresh cream
1 tsp dried thyme

1. Rinse the turkey under running water and remove the neck and insides. Boil these and the chicken wings in ample water. Let the turkey strain well, salt and pepper inside and out. Place the bunch of herbs inside the turkey, then stitch it close and tie its legs with a string.
2. In a bowl add the rosemary, marjoram, thyme, savory, olive oil, coarse grain salt, and a little pepper. Use this mixture to brush the turkey all over so that the herbs and grains of salt stick to its skin.
3. Place the turkey in a baking pan, chest up. Pour 2 cups of the stock over the turkey. Place the pan at the bottom rack of the oven preheated at 180ºC. Roast at 200ºC for 50 minutes, then cover the turkey in foil, lower heat to 180ºC and let the turkey on the grill for one more hour.
4. Remove the foil, pour one more cup from the stock and grill for 40 more minutes, then remove turkey from the oven, place it in a large dish, cover it with foil and let it "rest" for 25 minutes before curving.
5. In the meanwhile, prepare the sauce: Collect the juice from the baking pan and strain it in a bowl to set it aside. Pick a second bowl and pour in the brandy where you dissolve the flour and work with a fork to make a fine "paste". Melt the butter in a saucepan and stir in the thyme, add the collected juice, two cups from the stock, and the "paste" of brandy and flour. Mix well with a wooden spoon until the mixture coagulates. Then pour in the fresh cream, a little pepper and salt.
6. Serve the turkey pieces, sauce and green salad.

PORK SMOKED WITH 3 HERBS

Serves 8
1 pork shoulder with bone, 2 kg
1 bunch of dried oregano
1 bunch of dried sage
1 bunch of dried thyme
lemon leaves
salt

1. Roughly cut the pork shoulder into slices and sprinkle with salt. Let slices rest for 8-10 hours. Subsequently, arrange the pieces on grill in the oven and place below the grill a baking pan with water to catch the melting fat. Grill at 200ºC for 30 minutes, then lower heat at 180ºC and continue grilling for at least one hour and ten minutes.

2. When the pork slices are golden brown, remove the baking pan below the grill and carefully dispose of its contents. Place the chopped herbs in a fire-proof earthenware in the place of the baking pan and light up the herbs with a match (turn off the main power switch first). Let them burn for 1-2 minutes, then blow fire out. The smoke emitted will provide an excellent scent to the pork slices.

3. On a flat surface arrange 2-3 baking sheets side by-side, spread the lemon leaves and the hot pork slices on top of them. Wrap the meat pieces well and let them cool off for 1 hours. Serve with a lot of salad.

CHICKEN WITH A CRUST OF HERBS

Serves 8
4 small chicken
60 gr whole meal flour
1 tsp dried thyme, ground
1 tsp dried marjoram, ground
1 lemon, grated rind
freshly ground black pepper
2 tsp dried thyme
2 tsp dried marjoram
1 egg, whisked
60 gr butter

1. Preheat oven at 200ºC. Pour the flour in a bowl and stir in well the ground herbs, half the grated lemon rinds and pepper.

2. Insert half a teaspoon of the above mixture and a slice of lemon inside each chicken. Close the chicken breasts tight. Brush each chicken with the whisked egg and flour them with 3/4 of the flour quantity.

3. Melt the butter in a baking pan in the oven. Arrange the chicken in the baking pan and brush them with the butter. Let them cook at 180ºC for 30 minutes. Open the oven window and slide out the baking pan. Brush the chicken with butter once more and sprinkle them with the rest of the flour. Push back the baking pan and continue cooking for 15 more minutes, or until a fine golden crust forms on each chicken.

FISH FILLET WITH MINT AND CORIANDER

Serves 6
1 large fish fillet (grouper, sea bream, or perch)
1 tbsp crushed coriander
3 cloves garlic
1 tbsp mint, finely chopped
1 tsp sweet paprika
½ kg yogurt
½ cup olive oil
salt
pepper

1. For the marinade: whisk the eggs, yogurt, olive oil, garlic, mint and all herbs in a bowl.
2. Spread the fish fillet in a deep dish and use the above mixture to marinade the fish for an hour. Remove the fillets from the marinade and tap slightly dry with kitchen paper.

Place fillets on charcoal or oven grill for 20-30 minutes, until brown on both sides. Make sure that the fillets retain their juice.

PENNE WITH AROMATIC HERBS

Serves 6
1 packet of penne (pasta)
2 egg plants
1 large onion ground roughly
1 clove garlic
4 courgettes, sliced 1 cm thick
2 fresh, peeled and finely chopped tomatoes
1 tbsp sugar
salt
pepper
1/3 cup olive oil
½ tsp dried basil
½ tsp dried thyme
½ tsp dried oregano
grated hard cheese ("kefalotyri")

1. Preheat oven at 200ºC.
2. Peel and cube the egg-plants. Toss them in a bowl with salted water (not much salt). Allow them to rest for one hour, then remove, rinse and pat them dry. Arrange the egg-plants in a baking pan along with all ingredients, but not the cheese.
3. Bake in the oven for 20-30 minutes, or until a little brown.
4. Boil the penne for 7-8 minutes, strain them in a colander and mix them in a bowl with the hot vegetables, cheese and freshly grated cheese. Serve immediately.

Smoked pork with oregano, sage and thyme.

PASTA WITH HERBS

1 tbsp sage
1 tbsp rosemary
1 tbsp oregano
1 tbsp thyme
1 tbsp chervil
1 tbsp marjoram or basil
3 eggs
2 3/4 cups flour or semolina
1 tbsp olive oil
cold water, if necessary

1. Mix the spices with the herbs. Whisk the eggs with the olive oil and slowly add the flour to make a lump of dough (add a little cold water if necessary).
2. Kneed the dough for 15 minutes and let it rest to rise for 15 minutes. Shape the dough into a roll and dust it with flour. Kneed it again. Repeat this process 6 to 8 times.
3. Pass the dough through a pastry cutter and cut dough into strips at the thickness you prefer by adjusting the machine cutters.
4. Alternatively, you can shape the dough strips by hand. To do so, cut little dough pieces in long and thin strips as in fettuccini, or thicker as in lasagna, cannelloni, ravioli, etc.
5. When working with the dough, make sure you use the correct quantity of flour so that dough does not stick on the pastry board.

MARINATED OLIVES WITH THYME AND FENNEL

3 cups assorted olives, (rinsed and dried)
1 cup extra virgin olive oil
4 sprigs fresh thyme
1 ½ tsp fennel seeds
the rind from 2 oranges (2 coils)
1/4 tsp dried hot pepper (flakes)
1 laurel leaf
1 clove garlic, finely chopped
1/4 cup lemon juice

1. Place the olives in a large bowl.
2. Pour the olive oil in a little saucepan and stir in the thyme, fennel seeds, orange peel, pepper flakes, laurel leaf and garlic. Warm all at low heat for 30 minutes.
3. Mix the olives with the oil and herbs. Also pour the lemon juice over the olives and close the glass jar. Shake the jar vigorously to mix the herbs

   with the olives well.
4. Let the jar cool off at room temperature, then refrigerate it for 10 days. Bring the olives at room temperature before serving; strain most of the olive oil.

HERB OMELET

Serves 6
10 eggs
2 tbsp flour, all purpose
5 tbsp hard, salted cheese, grated
2 ½ tbsp fresh mint
5 tbsp olive oil
salt
pepper

1. Whisk the eggs in a bowl. Add the flour, cheese, mint, salt, and pepper and beat the mixture with a fork to mix ingredients well.
2. In a non-stick medium-size frying pan warm 1 tablespoon of olive oil. Pour in ½ cup of the egg mixture and cover the pan with a lid.
3. Fry this omelet for 3 minutes, both sides, and remove it from the heat as soon as done (crispy top).
4. Repeat the same process with one more ½ cup of the mixture, until you are satisfied with the number of omelets produced or until you exhaust the mixture.
5. Shape each little omelet into rolls and serve them on a flat dish over lettuce leaves.

GREEK SALAD WITH MINT AND OREGANO

1 kg medium size tomatoes
2 small cucumbers
2 green peppers
1 medium size red onion
175 gr feta cheese
125 gr kalamata olives or other Greek olives

for the Vinaigrette:
3-5 sprigs of fresh mint
3-5 sprigs of fresh oregano
7-10 sprigs of parsley
3 tbsp vinegar (from red wine)
salt
pepper
125 ml extra virgin olive oil

1. Make the vinaigrette with the aromatic ingredients. Pluck the leaves of mint and oregano from the stems and chop them roughly.

Mint goes well with carrots, peas, corn and delicious thinly sliced tomato salad.

2. In a little bowl, mix and beat the vinegar, salt and pepper. Whisk in the olive oil gradually to make a slightly thick mixture. Add the chopped spices then whisk the sauce again. Test for salt and pepper.

3. Prepare the vegetables. Remove the stems from the tomatoes and cut them in small slices. Peel and chop the cucumbers in thin slices.
4. With pointed knife remove the stems from the peppers with an incision round the perimeter of the stem. Halve and deseed the peppers. Place them on a flat surface with open half top and slice longitudinally in strips. Slice strips in squares.
5. Peel and chop the onion in thin rings. Separate rings with your fingers.
6. Pick the feta cheese and cut out slices approximately 1.25 cm wide each. Stack the cheese slices and cut them into little cubes Toss the tomatoes, cucumbers, peppers, and cheese in a large salad bowl. Whisk the vinaigrette vigorously and pour it over the Greek salad.
7. Use two spoons to mix the ingredients with the vinaigrette in the bowl, add the olives and feta cheese and work gently with the spoons again. Taste for salt and pepper.

SALAD WITH GRAPES AND GREENS

for a large salad bowl
250 gr rocket
250 gr endives
250 gr spinach
2 carrots
30 grapes
4-5 radishes
3 tbsp vinegar
1 tbsp mustard
2 tbsp olive oil
salt
pepper

1. Choose the most tender parts from all vegetables and toss them in a large salad bowl.
2. Grate the carrots, radishes and add them in the salad bowl. Spread the grapes over the salad and refrigerate.
3. Place the olive oil, vinegar, mustard, salt and pepper in a mixer and process well to make the dressing. Pour the dressing over the salad.

PICKLED GREEN PEPPERS AND CABBAGE

1 kg green peppers
1 cabbage (medium size), finely chopped
1 tbsp salt (for massaging the cabbage)
2 carrots, medium size, chopped
4-5 cloves garlic, crushed
1 ½ cup fennel
1 cup finely chopped parsley

for the juice:
2 lt clear water
40-50 gr salt
1-2 tsp red pepper flakes

1. Rinse the peppers under running water and open them from the bottom with a cutting incision, the size of a carrot slice. "Uncork" pepper pulling by the stem and use your fingers to deseed and clear the insides. Finely chop the cabbage and rub it with the salt. Fill in the peppers with the finely chopped carrots, greens, parsley, and greens. "Cork" the pepper back with carrot slices and arrange

the peppers in glass jars; inserting cloves of garlic among them.

2. Bring the water to boil well and let it cool off. Add the salt and pepper in the water, stir to dissolve well, then fill the jars with water to top the peppers. Store the jars in a cool place around the house. Do not seal the jars well for the pickled peppers to mature. The gas formed inside the jars needs to come out. It takes approximately 6-7 days for the pickled peppers to start maturing. They start by getting slightly yellow. Now, its time to seal the jars well and store them in the refrigerator, otherwise contents will go sour.

QUINCE IN THE OVEN WITH SPICES

3 large quinces, peeled and halved
1 quince, peeled and finely grated
1 cup sweet wine
2 tbsp "raki" or "ouzo"
1 tbsp honey
8 cloves
1 tsp cinnamon
the juice from 2 lemons

1. Peel, halve and deseed the quinces and toss them in a bowl of cold water where you will have previously added the juice from two lemons.

2. Preheat the oven at 200oC. Strain the quinces well and arrange them in a pyrex dish and stick a clove on them. Sprinkle with the sugar, grated quince and cinnamon. Slightly warm the wine and dissolve it in the warm honey. Pour this over the quinces, do the same with the "raki"/"ouzo" and cover the quinces with foil.

3. Place the pyrex dish with the quinces in the oven and bake at 180oC for approximately 60 minutes. Remove the foil and allow the quinces to brown for 10 more minutes. Serve them with a tablespoon of yogurt or whisked fresh cream.

FIGS WITH HONEY AND SPICES

10-15 dried figs
1 cinnamon (small bark)
3 cloves
1 laurel leaf
1 tsp honey
1 cup almonds, blanched
1 cup thyme (tea)

1. Empty the thyme tea in a saucepan, add the laurel leaf, figs, cinnamon, cloves and honey. Add two cups of water and simmer for 6-8 minutes.

2. Cover the saucepan with its lid and continue simmering until the figs get tender and soak well in the spiced juice.

3. Serve them with their syrup and almonds.

GREEK PANCAKES WITH ASSORTMENT OF HERBS

250 gr white flour
60 gr corn flour
60 gr milk
2 egg yolks, whisked
2 cloves garlic, crushed
2 tbsp fresh/dried mint
2 tbsp fresh/dried oregano
1 tbsp fresh/dried marjoram
1 tbsp fresh/dried basil
1 tbsp fresh/dried thyme
olive oil (for frying)
salt
pepper
4-5 tbsp yogurt

1. In a bowl stir in the white flour, corn flour, milk and whisked egg yolks and cover bowl for half an hour.
2. Add the herbs, garlic, salt and pepper in the bowl and stir well.
3. Warm the olive oil in a deep frying pan and spoon in 2-3 tablespoons of the above mixture. A pancake starts forming. Fry until the pancakes are slightly brown on both sides. Remove each pancake using a perforated spoon and place them on large dish covered with kitchen paper to absorb remaining olive oil. Serve with yogurt.

BREAD WITH MARJORAM AND ROSEMARY

500 gr white flour
35 gr fresh yeast
1 tbsp white wine
2 tbsp extra virgin olive oil
2 tbsp rosemary, marjoram, finely chopped
sea salt, coarse grain

1. Put the flour into a bowl; make a cavity in the middle of the flour "dune" and add the yeast (dissolved in ½ cup of tepid water), the wine, olive oil and a tablespoon of herbs.
2. Start working with the mixture, adding a little tepid water to gradually get a smooth dough. When you are satisfied with its texture, let the dough rest for 10-15 minutes.
3. Use this dough to roll a pastry sheet 1 ½ cm thick, which you spread in a square baking pan with slightly buttered bottom.
4. Sprinkle with ample coarse grain sea salt and the herbs. Bake at 200ºC for 35-40 minutes. Serve at room temperature.

BRIOCHE WITH HERBS

300 gr flour
170 gr butter in room temperature
4 eggs
15 gr yeast
1 tsp sugar
½ tsp salt
½ tsp marjoram, finely chopped
1 tsp oregano
½ tsp green pepper, roughly chopped

1. Empty the flour in a bowl and make a hole in the middle. Dissolve the yeast in tepid water and pour it in the hole, then the butter, eggs, sugar, salt, pepper, marjoram and oregano.
2. Work with your hands to make a dough with this mixture. When done, cover the dough with a cotton towel and let it rest until it doubles in size.
3. Brush the bottom of baking tin for brioche with butter, put the dough in, cover and let it rest for 15-20 minutes. Brush the surface of the dough with the whisked egg.
4. Place the baking tin in the oven and bake at 180ºC for 20 minutes. Raise the heat to 200ºC and continue for 20 more minutes.

Baked half quince with a caramelized crust
and a pinch of cinnamon.

BREAD WITH RAISINS AND ORANGE

1 kg hard flour
350 gr raisins
3 tbsp orange rind, grated
3 tsp dry yeast
150 gr sugar
1 tsp salt
3/4 of water glass tepid milk
3 tbsp olive oil

1. In a bowl dissolve the yeast in the milk with a teaspoon of sugar. Stir well and cover the bowl.
2. In a kneading bowl or mixer bowl pour in the flour, stir in the sugar, salt and grated orange rinds. Pour in the foamy yeast from the first bowl and start kneading. Use any tepid water it takes to produce a soft and elastic dough. When done, toss in the raisins, which you have previously wetted and dried well. Knead to mix the ingredients well. Finally, add the olive oil and kneed again to absorb mix well.
3. Cover the dough and let it rest for half an hour. Then pick enough dough to kneed little loaves which you place in oblong cake tins or large baking pan, both lined with greaseproof paper. Cover tin/pan with two napkins and let loaves rise.
4. When the loaves are double in volume, brush top with milk or egg albumin whisked in tepid water. Stab loaves at places and bake in preheated oven at 175ºC for approximately 1 hour.

HERBS MARMALADE

(accompanies cold dishes, pies or cheese)

1 kg green apples, sliced
500 gr sugar per 500 ml of juice
30 gr herbs, freshly chopped (mint, basil, marjoram, rosemary)
the juice from one lemon
1/4 cup vinegar (from apples)

1. Cook apple slices in ample water until they get tender.
2. When done, remove the apples from the pan and place them in muslin cloth and let them drain their juice overnight. Make sure and note the amount of juice drained.
3. In a fresh pan pour in the juice, add the sugar and warm at low heat to dissolve. Secure the herbs in a muslin pouch and insert pouch in the pan;

add the lemon juice and vinegar. Bring the contents to the boil and then simmer until the marmalede is thick.

4. Remove the pouch from the pan and transfer the marmalade to warm, sterilized jars. Do not cover jars until marmalade has cooled down. Then insert the sprigs of fresh and dried herbs and seal the jars.

SAUCE WITH OLIVE OIL, MINT, MUSTARD AND OREGANO

(for boiled eggs)

½ cup extra virgin olive oil
2 tbsp vinegar
1 tsp mint, finely chopped
1 tsp oregano
1 tsp mustard
1 tbsp flour
1 tsp salt (not completely filled)
2-3 drops tepid water

1. Mix the ingredients in a deep bowl and whisk them to a liquid mass.
2. Cover the bowl with transparent film and refrigerate for 45-50 minutes. Use this sauce to dress hard boiled eggs.

FENNEL SAUCE

1 fennel bulb, finely chopped
3 tbsp butter
1 tbsp extra virgin olive oil
1 cup dried white wine
½ cup milk

1. In a saucepan put the fennel, two tablespoons of butter, the olive oil and a little water and cover saucepan with lid. Add the wine and cook at low temperature until the fennel is tender.
2. Transfer the contents of the saucepan into a food-processor bowl and add the butter and milk. Process the contents of the bowl to fine pulp. Return the pulp to the saucepan and gently warm them up. Empty the contents in a saucebowl and serve.

PESTO WITH BASIL, MINT AND ORANGE

3/4 cup extra virgin olive oil
1 cup fresh basil, finely chopped
½ cup fresh mint, finely chopped
½ cup nuts
2 tbsp grated fresh orange rind
2 cloves garlic
½ tsp salt
½ tsp green pepper

1. Place the nuts, basil, mint, garlic in a blender and purée to form a smooth paste.
2. As you work with the blender, slowly pour in the olive oil, grated orange rind, salt, and pepper. Stop the operation of the blender as soon as the olive oil has been absorbed. Test the purée; if too thick, add 1-2 tablespoons of olive oil and process for 2-3 more minutes.

PESTO WITH PARSLEY AND CAPERS

1 tbsp breadcrumbs (scraped out of one-day old / cottage bread)
$1/4$ cup vinegar (from red wine)
$1/4$ cup parsley, finely chopped
salt
freshly ground pepper
1 hard boiled egg, thinly sliced
1 tbsp capers, strained and chopped
2 cups extra virgin olive oil

1. Soak the breadcrumbs in the vinegar for 10 minutes. Pick the soaking breadcrumbs in your hand and squeeze them dry.
2. Mix these breadcrumbs with parsley, salt, pepper, egg slices and capers, add the olive oil and mix well with a spoon again.
3. Place the pesto in a salad bowl and serve.

PESTO A LA GENOVEZE FOR PASTA DISHES

1 handful of basil leaves, rinsed well
1 clove garlic
30 gr pine seeds
30 gr hard cheese ("kefalotyri"), ground
30 gr pecorino cheese, ground
1 $1/2$ cup of extra virgin olive oil
1 tsp salt

1. Put the basil leaves, garlic and pine seeds in a food processor bowl and process. Transfer the mixture into a soup tureen and add the hard cheese, perocino cheese and salt.
2. Stir in the olive oil slowly to make a fine cream.

AROMATIC OLIVE OIL WITH GARLIC, LAUREL AND ROSEMARY

Extra virgin olive oil
3 cloves garlic
6 small laurel leaves
2 sprigs rosemary
6 toothpicks
1 empty bottle

1. Peel and halve the cloves of garlic. Thread the laurel leaves and garlic halves per toothpick and insert them into the bottle.
2. Also, insert the rosemary sprigs into the bottle, fill in with extra virgin olive oil and seal the bottle.

VINAIGRETTE WITH HERBS

½ cup fresh parsley leaves
1 tbsp fresh basil leaves
$1/4$ cup fresh oregano leaves
1 cup extra virgin olive oil
2 tbsp lemon juice
2 tbsp white vinegar (from wine)
1 clove garlic, crushed
1 cup shallots or onion springs, chopped
1 tsp French mustard
salt
pepper
1 tbsp honey

1. Finely chop all the herbs and place them in glass jar that seals well.

You will be surprised at the simplicity of this sweet!! Figs soaked in a syrup of honey, thyme tea, cinnamon sticks and cloves.

2. Add the rest of the ingredients, seal the jar and shake vigorously to mix well.

3. Refrigerate the dressing. If, per chance, the olive oil coagulates, remove the jar from the refrigerator and store it in a cool place at room temperature.

FOUR SPICES VINEGAR

1 kg vinegar
2 cloves garlic
1 onion
1 pinch of thyme
1 bunch parsley
1 sprig rosemary
a few sage leaves
5 pepper corns
1 laurel leaf

1. Boil the ingredients for 5 minutes and then strain to collected the scented vinegar. Pour the vinegar in a bottle after it has cooled down. Alternatively, instead of boiling the herbs and spices, pour the hot vinegar over the ingredients, cover the container and set it aside for 10 minutes for the contents to cool off; then strain and pour the vinegar in a bottle.

VINEGAR WITH HONEY AND HERBS

3 cups cider vinegar
2 cloves garlic, sliced
½ cup honey
2 tsp dried oregano
1 tsp dried mint
1 tsp dried thyme
sprigs of fresh thyme, for bottling

1. Simmer all ingredients, excepting the fresh thyme, for 6-7 minutes. Do not use an aluminum vessel. Let the mixture cool off.

2. Strain the mixture first through a cotton cloth and then through a coffee filter to collect the juice.

3. Transfer the contents into clean glass bottles and add the sprigs of fresh thyme, seal and store the bottles for 3 weeks before use.

VINEGAR WITH LAUREL, THYME AND SAGE

4 cups vinegar
2 laurel leaves
1 tsp thyme
1 tsp sage

1. Pick a clean and large bottle neck bottle to insert the aromatic herbs and vinegar. Seal the bottle well and store it in a cool place in the house for 2-3 weeks.

2. Transfer the vinegar to a clean bottle and dispose of the aromatic herbs.

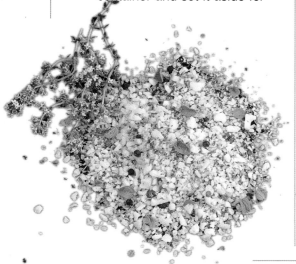

A mixture of herbs and spices with coarse sea salt.

A painter's pallet of colour and taste. Sauces and dips made from capers, basil, thyme, oregano, roses and mint.

VINEGAR SCENTED WITH ROSEMARY AND PINK PEPPER

2 cups vinegar
1 sprig rosemary
1 tsp black ground pepper

1. Rinse the rosemary under running water and tap it dry with kitchen paper, then insert it in a bottle along with the pepper. Fill the bottle with vinegar and seal well.
2. Store in a cool place around the house for 3 weeks before use.

MAYONNAISE WITH GREEN HERBS

2 tbsp vinegar from apples
1 egg yolk
1 whole egg
2 cups of French mustard
2 tbsp fresh basil leaves
2 tbsp fresh oregano leaves
salt
black pepper
1 tsp sugar
1/4 cup yogurt

1. Place the vinegar, egg yolk, hard boiled egg, and mustard in the blender and process for 10 seconds.
2. Finely chop the herbs, empty them in the processor bowl along with the salt, pepper and sugar and process for 5 more seconds. While the blender is in operation, gradually add the olive oil to produce a thick and smooth purée.
3. Add more olive oil to adjust thickness. While the blender is in operation, slowly spoon in the yogurt. When done with the yogurt, process for a couple of seconds.
4. Place the mayonnaise in a jar, seal with acid-proof lid and refrigerate before use.

BOUQUE GARNI
(assortment of herbs for soups, boiled meat and fish)

1 laurel leaf
1 sprig thyme
1 sprig parsley
1 sprig celery

1. Fasten them neatly into a bunch or wrap and secure them in muslin cloth. You can insert them to impart their particular scent to stock/soup, fish and meats.

ZA' ATAR
(Lebanese herb mixture for bread)

2 tbsp thyme (ground to powder)
1 tbsp sumac
1 tsp sesame, roasted
½ tsp marjoram (ground to powder)
2 tbsp olive oil

Mix all herbs and spices with the olive oil. Use this paste to rub Arab style pies or bread. You can also mix this paste with dough to make bread.

Herbs always impart a unique taste to breads, brioche, cakes and biscuits.

MIXED HERBS FOR RICE DISHES

Serves 8
20 gr dried rose petals
1 piece of cinnamon bark
20 gr cardamom seeds
6-8 strands of saffron
50 gr almonds

Mix all herbs and spices with almonds in a mortar bowl. Crush them into powder and then use this to serve with rice.

HERBS BLEND FOR CHICKEN OR TURKEY

1 tsp thyme
1 tsp oregano
½ tsp cumin
½ tsp black pepper
1 tsp salt

Mix all ingredients and use mixture to sprinkle over or inside chicken or turkey.

HERBAL MARINADE FOR KEBAB ON GRILL

1 tsp mint, freshly chopped
2-3 strands of saffron
½ tsp dill
1 clove garlic, finely chopped
2 tbsp olive oil
3 tbsp white wine
½ tsp salt

1. Mix the ingredients and add the olive oil, wine and let the mixture rest for 2-3 hours in room temperature.
2. Use this mixture to brush kebab.

HERBAL DRINKS

SWEET TEA WITH SAGE, THYME AND HONEY

½ lt water
1 tbsp sage
1 tsp thyme
¾ cup "raki" or "tsipouro"
4-5 tbsp honey
5 pepper seeds

1. Boil water in a pan and then add the sage and thyme. Let them boil for 4 minutes.
2. Remove the pan from fire, strain and collect the tea, add the "raki"/"tsipouro" and the honey. Stir well to dissolve the honey and boil the mixture for 3 more minutes. Server the tea hot.

MALLOW CHAMOMILE, LIME LEAVES, ANISE AND HONEY

1 tsp mallow flowers
1tsp chamomile flowers
1 tsp lime (flowers and leave)
1 tbsp honey

1. Pour 5-6 cups of water in a heavy bottom pan. Slightly warm the water, vigorously stir in the honey and bring the mixture to the boil.
2. Remove the pan from fire, add the herbs and cover with lid.

Let the drink rest for 10 minutes and then strain to collect it.
3. Serve hot and test for sweetness; add more honey or sugar if required.

GREEN TEA AND MINT

2 tbsp green tea
6 tbsp sugar
1 handful of fresh mint leaves
6 cups of boiled water
orange rinds or 1 tsp orange blossomwater

1. Pour the green tea in a teapot and add the sugar, mint leaves and orange rinds or blossomwater. Boil water in a kettle, then bring the kettle over the mixture and pour in the hot water. Stir the mixture and let it infuse for 10-15 minutes.
2. For a fizzy drink, take one cup of tea from the teapot and pour it back raising the cup gradually as you pour the tea in the teapot. To increase the fizziness of your drink, pour the tea from the teapot into your teacup from a height of approximately 30 cm.

ROSE SERBET

600 ml cold water
450 gr sugar
2 tbsp lemon juice
4 tbsp rosewater
2 cups rose petals

1. Mix the sugar, lemon juice and water in a container and let the mixture rest for 2 days. Then bring the mixture to the boil.
2. Lower the heat to simmer until the mixture turns thick. The mixture is ready when a thin film sticks to the back side of the spoon. (if you use food colouring, add them at this stage).
3. Stir in the rose water and simmer for 2-3 more minutes. Let the syrup cool off inside the container. Then pour it in an airtight jar or bottle. Store the blend in a cool place and keep it refrigerated after first use.
4. Dissolve 1 tablespoon in cold water and serve as is or with ice cubes.

REFRESHING DRINK WITH LEMON AND MINT

Serves 1
4 sprigs of mint
½ tsp sugar
crushed ice
½ tsp lemon juice
2 tbsp grapefruit juice
½ cup iced tonic
lemon slices (wedges) to garnish

1. Crush 2 sprigs of mint with the sugar and transfer them to a water glass. Fill the glass with the crushed iced.
2. Add the lemon juice, grapefruit juice and tonic. Stir carefully and garnish with the remaining mint sprigs and lemon wedges.

A refreshing beverage made from yogurt, mint, salt, ice and a bitter thyme liquor.

ROSE - HONEY

*10 cups of fresh or dried fragrant
rose petals
2 lt of boiled water
1 kg honey*

1. Empty the rose petals in a bowl. Pour in the boiled water, cover the bowl for 10 hours and then collect the juice by straining through a fine colander.
2. Mix the juice with the honey, empty the contents in a container and simmer for 1-2 hours. Occasionally skim the froth. Transfer the juice in jars and store in a cool place.

ROSE FRUITS, ELDER AND ORANGE RIND

*1 tbsp fruits of roses
1 tsp elder flowers
a piece orange skin
1 tsp honey*

1. Warm 5-6 cups of water in a pot and spoon in the honey. Mix vigorously and bring the mixture to the boil.
2. Remove the container from the oven ring, add the herbs and orange skin and cover the container with its lid. Let the drink rest for 10 minutes, then strain. Serve with additional honey or sugar.

QUINCE TEA

*1 lt water
dry skins from 4 quinces
1 small cinnamon bark
3 carnation cloves
sugar or honey*

1. As soon as you bring the water to the boil, add the quince skins and simmer for 4-5 minutes. Add the spices and continue simmering for 30 seconds more.
2. Remove the container from the oven ring and let it rest for 2 minutes before straining. Serve as is or with honey/sugar.

"KARTERAKI" DRINK (HERBAL BLEND TEA)

*½ tsp sage
1 tsp marjoram
1 tsp dittany (dictamus)
½ tsp chamomile*

1. Mix the herbs in a bowl.
2. Soak them in 4 cups of warm (70ºC) water. Cover the bowl with a flat dish and let the drink rest for 10 minutes. Strain and serve immediately.

SAGE AND ROSES INFUSION

Serves 4
1 tbsp chamomile
2 tbsp dried petals of wild, fragrant roses

1. Bring to the boil 5 cups of
   water. Leave until the infusion has stopped boiling for 4 minutes.
   Spoon in the leaves and cover the container.
2. Strain the drink 8 minutes later
   and serve immediately.

YOGURT AND MINT REFRESHMENT

Serves 6
1 cup of chilled water
1 cup chilled yogurt (Greek style)
½ tsp salt
1 tsp fresh mint (spearmint) leaves

1. Process the water and yogurt
   in a blender along with the salt. Just before you stop the
   processing add the mint slightly crushed.
2. Serve in tall glass with 1-2 tbsp of
   crushed ice or ice cubes and garnish with mint leaves.

Sage tea, warm and therapeutic, was favoured by the ancient Greeks as the elixir of youth.

LIQUOR

LIQUOR SCENTED WITH HERBS

3 sprigs thyme
3 sprigs rosemary
1 lemon sprig
6 sage leaves
6 mint leaves
2 1/4 cups dry anisette liquor
2 1/4 cups sweet anisette liquor
the rind from 1/2 orange, washed,
tapped dry and sliced in strips

1. Place the unwashed herbs in a dry and clean jar. Add the two anisette liquors and orange strips in the jar and seal it. Store away the jar in a dark, cool place for two months.
2. Strain the contents of the jar in a fine colander. Transfer the herbs to a clean bottle and pour in the juice you have previously strained and collected. Seal the bottle well.
3. Serve when needed

ROSE PETALS LIQUOR

250 gr red rose petal (approx. 24 roses)
2 1/2 cups confectioner's glaze

1 cup water
1 tsp coriander seeds
2 1/4 "raki" or vodka

1. Pluck the rose petals and remove the white tip that joins the calyx.
2. Add the water and sugar in a saucepan and warm for 5 minutes to make the syrup. Add the rose petals and coriander seeds. Boil for 5 more minutes then remove pan from oven ring and cover it with lid until the mixture cools off.
3. Pour the juice into a clean airtight jar through a fine sieve and add the "raki" or vodka. Seal the jar and store it in a cool place for a month.
4. Filter the juice and transfer it to a clean bottle

THYME AND SAVORY LIQUOR

For a small jar:
1 tbsp fresh thyme (floured tops)
1 tsp savory
2 cloves
1 tbsp honey
3 tbsp sugar
1/2 lt brandy

GRAPE SYRUP

3 ½ kg black grapes (ripe and firm)
900 gr sugar
1 ½ lt water
the skin from 1 lemon
a few tender vine leaves

1.   Rinse the grapes under running water. Use a pair of scissors to separate the fruits from the stalk but retain approximately only 1 mm from their stem. Collect 3 kg of grapes and spread them on a clean cloth and place them under the sun to dry for about an hour.
2.   In the meantime prepare the syrup: place the water, sugar and lemon skin in a saucepan to boil for 2 minutes. Then let the mixture cool off.
3.   Carefully select only those grapes that are whole and place them in jars. Insert a piece of lemon rind and two vine leaves per jar. Pour in the syrup to fill 3/4 of each jar. Seal jars well and sterilize for 15-20 minutes.
4.   Store jars in a cool, dark and dry place.

SAFFRON AND HERBS DRINK

1 ½ raki / tsipouro / vodka / grapa
500 gr sugar
5 (0.20 gr) saffron strands
1 tsp dried coriander
1 tsp cloves
2 small pieces of cinnamon bark
1 whole nutmeg

1.   Gather the herbs (coriander, cinnamon, nutmeg) together and wrap them in a cloth. Place the wrapped spices in a glass jar, fill in with raki and store the jar for 40 days. Shake the jar occasionally.
2.   Boil the sugar in a glass of water and as soon as the syrup cools off, mix it with the raki. Add more syrup to the raki, if required.
3.   Before transferring the drink into bottles, add the saffron strands to get the best out of their beneficial qualities and a nice colour for your drink.

1. Insert the unwashed thyme and savory in a jar.
2. Boil the honey, sugar, and cloves into the brandy for 2-3 minutes
3. Empty the boiled mixture into the jar and seal well.
4. Store in a cool and dark place for 20 days. Use this liquor to flavour warm drinks / infusions.

MINT LIQUOR

For a large bottle:
4 bunches of fresh mint
½ lt raki or vodka
½ lt ouzo
2 large nutmegs
2 small mastic pieces
4 cloves
2 cups sugar

1. Rinse the mint in running water the day before use and let it dry well.
2. Insert the mint bunches, mastic pieces, nutmeg, and sugar in a large neck bottle.
3. Seal the bottle and place it under direct sunlight for 12-15 days. Occasionally shake the bottle gently.
4. By the end of the 15-day period pour the ouzo in the bottle and store under sunlight for a month.
5. Subsequently pass the drink through a fine cloth into a clean bottle and store in a dark, cool place.

QUINCES LIQUOR

4 quinces chopped in four
1 ½ cup sugar
2 small cinnamon barks
5 cups excellent quality vodka

1. Wash the quinces well and wipe them dry with a towel. Quarter the quinces without peeling them.
2. Place the quince pieces in a food processor bowl and turn on/off the switch a couple of times for rough processing.
3. Empty the contents of the bowl into a large neck bottle and add the sugar, cinnamon and vodka.
4. Strain the contents through a sieve and into several smaller bottles and store them in a cool, dark place for 45 days.
5. Keep the liquor refrigerated.

FIGS IN BRANDY

3 kg of ripe figs
1 ½ sugar
300 gr walnuts, shelled
2 lemons, skins
½ lt brandy
1/3 cup warm water

1. Briefly rinse the figs and place them on burlap cloth to dry in the sun for about one hour.
2. Squeeze open (do not halve) each fig to insert 1/4 walnut, close and then place the figs in a glass jar in layers. Sprinkle each layer with a little sugar (make sure that 300 gr of sugar is enough for all layers), a small piece of lemon rind, a few drops of lemon juice and brandy. When the top layer is approximately 1 cm bellow the rim of the jar, add a few tablespoons of boiled water for the syrup.
3. Tightly seal the jar and sterilize for 3/4 of an hour. Store the jars in a cool, dark and dry place.

ROSE PETALS IN WINE

10 cups of white wine (unresinated)
2 cups of rose petals

1. Bring the wine to the boil and toss in the rose petals. Cover container with a lid for 2-3 hours. Strain, collect and keep the juice in a cool place.
2. Serve this juice as a warm tonic.

SAGE IN SWEET WINE

3 tbsp sage
1 lt sweet wine
1 cinnamon bark, small
2 cumin seeds

1. Boil the wine in stainless steel saucepan for 5 minutes. Add the sage, cinnamon, and cumin. Cove the pot and boil for 3 more minutes.
2. Transfer the contents of the pot to a clean container, seal well and let it rest for 10 days.
3. Strain, collect and store the wine at room temperature.

WINE WITH ROSEMARY AND THYME

2 lt red wine
2 large sprigs of fresh rosemary
1 tsp sage
1 tsp thyme
1 cinnamon bark
100 gr sugar

1. Pick a bottle with a wide neck to insert the herbs, add the sugar and pour in the wine. Seal the neck well and store for 8 days. In the meantime shake the bottle occasionally to dissolve the sugar.
2. Pass the mixture through a filter into a clean bottle and serve at room temperature.

MINT SORBET

2 cups of water
15 mint leaves
½ cup thick sugar syrup
3-4 fresh mint leaves (garnish)
3-4 thin lemon slices

1. Boil the mint leaves in two cups of water (60-70ºC). Cover the container and let it rest for 2 days.
2. Strain and add the syrup. Stir and allocate the sorbet to ice-cub holder. Place it in the freezer for at least 10 days before use.

3. Crush the cubs in a food processor. Transfer the crushed ice to the freezer.
4. Serve the sorbet in balls in tall glasses. Garnish with fresh mint and slices of lemon.

PUNCH WITH A BLEND OF HERBS

1 ½ lit red wine
1 cinnamon bark
3 cloves
½ tsp cress
½ cup sage infusion
½ cup marjoram infusion
½ cup thyme infusion
1 ½ tsp grated orange rinds
1 tsp grated lemon rinds
6 tbsp sugar
1 cup raisins
1 cup almonds, blanched and cut
1 tsp thyme or borage flowers
(garnish)

1. Boil the herbs and sugar in the wine over a spirit stove for 20 minutes. Add all the infusions, the grated orange and lemon rinds, raisins, almonds and stir well.
2. Let them simmer for 10 minutes.
3. Serve the punch warm and garnished with the thyme and borage flowers.

BASIC GREENS – HERBS – FRUIT
AND RELATED CULINARY APPLICATIONS

HERB	TASTE	USE
THYME Fresh or dried leaves	Bitter, sharp taste and aromatic	In all piquant dishes, bouquet garni, leeks, macaroni, and for aromatic vinegar.
POMEGRANATE Seeds, rind	Cool, aromatic, slightly styptic	Salads, sauces
GRAPES Leaves, fruit, sprouts	Cool, aromatic, sweet–citric	Sweets/Cakes, bread, salads, game.
QUINCE seeds	Very aromatic and styptic	Cakes, drinks, liquor, meat (pork)
LEEK Green section	Sweet and warm	Pies, soups, salads
CAPER fruit	Very piquant and sharp taste	In pasta, salads, pizzas, meat, eggs, fish and bread.
MALLOW Leaves, offshoots, flowers	Cool and sweet	Meat, drinks
ROCKET leaves	Sharp taste and pungent aroma	In salads with tomatoes, lettuce, wheat, fresh pasta.
NETTLE leaves	Cool, slightly bitter, styptic with no aroma	Pies, soups, risotto
PURSLANE leaves	Sweet, cool, sour without aroma	Salads, yogurt, chicken
ASPARAGUS Green section	Sweet, cool, without aroma	Salads, meat, soups
DICTAMUS Leaves, flowers	Sharp taste and aroma Slightly bitter	Drinks
ROSE, WILD Leaves, fruit	Sweet, styptic, aromatic Fruit – slightly sour	Sherbet, sweets, in condiments
FIGS Sweet, slightly aromatic	Sweet, slightly aromatic	Cakes, salads

BASIC GREENS – HERBS – FRUIT
AND RELATED CULINARY APPLICATIONS

HERB	TASTE	USE
POPPY Whole (green leaves) White or Blue (seeds)	Sweet, aromatic and slightly dry	Vegetable pies, bread making, biscuits, cakes
SAFFRON Whole (stamens)	Aromatic, slightly bitter	Adds colour to food, particularly in rice dishes, cakes, liquors, sweets
BASIL Fresh or dried leaves	Sweet, pungent and aromatic	In pesto sauces, raw or cooked tomatoes, eggplants, spaghetti, salads, fish, cheese.
DAPHNE (LAUREL) Fresh or dried leaves	Sweet, acute aroma and discrete taste	In bouquet garni, soups, stock, casserole, game, puddings.
BORAGE Leaves, flowers fresh	Cool taste, scentless and slightly moist	The leaves in salads, soups and pancakes (whole leaves). The flowers in refreshing wines, salads.
CHAMOMILE Dried flower heads	Sweet, discrete aroma	Teas, drinks
CHICORY Leaves, root Fresh or dried	Bitter, styptic	The leaves in salads; the root cooked as substitute of coffee; in casserole with meat.
FENNEL Leaves, sprigs, stems, seeds	Sharp, intense aroma, sweet	Fish, lamb, pork. In pies with wild herbs.
MARJORAM Fresh or dried leaves	Sharp taste, intense aroma, slightly bitter	In bouquet garni, widely used in meat and vegetable dishes, puddings and bread
SPEARMINT Fresh or dried leaves	Cool and aromatic	In sauces and condiments, yogurt, summer vegetables and fruit, teas, drinks and cakes.
OREGANO Fresh or dried leaves	Sharp taste and slightly bitter aroma	In meat and vegetable dishes, as stuffing and in pasta dishes, pizzas, meatballs, and bread.
ROSEMARY Fresh or dried leaves and sprigs	Bitter and dry with sharp taste and aroma	Lamb, pork, fish, poultry, potatoes, snails, wines. It adds aroma to vinegar and oil.
SAGE Fresh or dried leaves and sprigs	Slightly bitter, intense aroma	Red meat (pork), stuffing, sauces, sausages, eels, cheese, tea, apple juice, white beans
SAVORY Fresh or dried leaves	Intense aroma, pungent.	Red meat, eggs, bread

TABLE 1

Fat soluble vitamins

Vitamin A:
Carrots, garlic, onion, tomato, spinach, berries, orange, apricot, lemon, cereals, wheat seeds, milk, oil from fish liver, eggs, greens.
Vitamin D:
Oil from fish liver, milk, eggs, vegetables.
Vitamin E:
Cereals, water-cress, cabbage, peas, parsley and vegetable oils, particularly peanut oil; flour.
Vitamin K:
Potatoes, tomatoes, strawberries, spinach, peas, cabbage

TABLE 2

Water soluble vitamins

Vitamin B1:
Yeast, grain, rice, carrots, lettuce, spinach, tomatoes.
Vitamin B2:
Fresh beans, wheat seeds, turnip leaves, asparagus, especially in meat, eggs, and milk.
Vitamin B6:
Cereals (rice, barley, oats), soya, beans, walnuts.
Vitamin B12:
Vegetables, leek, cabbage root, celery.
Vitamin PP:
Peanuts, asparagus, wheat, whole grain corn, rice, yeast, parsley.
Vitamin P:
Fruits, whole grain corn, pepper, beet, cabbage, lettuce.
Vitamin C:
Orange, fruits, cabbage, radish, tomatoes, fresh beans, gooseberry.
Vitamin Bc:
Wheat, all green leaves, yeast
Vitamin B5:
Peanuts, mushrooms, wheat, whole grain rice, fruit, vegetables.
Vitamin H:
Cereals

TABLE 3

Minerals

Calcium
Rice, oats, barley, yeast, walnuts, yogurt, onions, peas, cabbage, carrots, tomatoes, maize, leek, apricot, pineapple, cherries, cheese, eggs.

Iron
Spinach, parsley, strawberries, celery, blackberries, bananas, pineapple, nuts, oranges, apricots, asparagus, rice, leek, eggs.

Phosphorus
Cereals, carrots, peas, soya, fruits, apricots, almonds, hazel-nuts, lettuce, onion, cheese, eggs.

Iodine
In some mineral waters, seaweed, pineapple, garlic, artichoke, onions, spinach, white beet.

Magnesium
Onions, cereals, fruits, apples, cherries, strawberries, grapes, plums, peaches, mandarin, sea-salt.

Potassium
Wheat, carrots, potatoes, tomatoes, peas, cherries, grapes, walnuts, hazel-nuts, apples, peanuts, fruits, strawberries.

Copper
Peas, gooseberries, figs, strawberries, dates, chestnuts, coconuts, oranges, blackberries.

Sodium
Kitchen salt, oranges, dates, cherries, chestnuts, peanuts, apples, peaches, spinach, lentils, carrots, strawberries.

Sulfur
Cabbages, onions, bananas, cherries, spinach, pears, fruits, sweet almonds, carrots, asparagus.